Queer Prophets

Queer Prophets

The Bible's Surprise Ending
to the Story of Sexuality and Gender

Greg Paul

WIPF & STOCK · Eugene, Oregon

QUEER PROPHETS
The Bible's Surprise Ending to the Story of Sexuality and Gender

Wipf & Stock
An Imprint of Wipf and Stock Publishers
199 W. 8th Ave., Suite 3
Eugene, OR 97401

www.wipfandstock.com

PAPERBACK ISBN: 978-1-7252-6656-8
HARDCOVER ISBN: 978-1-7252-6657-5
EBOOK ISBN: 978-1-7252-6658-2

Manufactured in the U.S.A.   09/25/20

For the peculiar prophets
who have kept me longing and searching for "a better truth"
and by their persons and presence have revealed to me
a more spacious truth,
a more glorious consummation,
and a greater Love than I had ever imagined.

Contents

Introduction

This Is a Story, Friend

THIS IS A STORY, friend, so pour yourself something to sip on and pull up a chair. You might say it's the story of a theological quest, but that seems a little bloodless, although it's true enough in a limited way. Really, it's the tale of one straight, pretty conservative Christian guy who kept looking for better answers because so many of his friends were LGTBQ2+. In the process he—I—realized that the narrative twist at the conclusion of the Bible story clarified much that had been obscure or downright problematic before. I had never heard anyone else reference this perspective before (still haven't), so after about six years of ruminating on it and testing the ideas out on friends, some of whom are in fact actual theologians, I thought I should put it out there.

I might just be bold enough to describe myself as a student of the Bible—I've been reading it almost daily for close to fifty years, since I was a child, and studying and preaching from it almost weekly in my own quirky way for more than forty—but I'm certainly no scholar. You should know that right out of the gate. I have zero formal academic theological training. On the other hand, I've spent decades trying to live the gospel on the streets of Toronto, the largest city in Canada. The specific area that I've worked in houses what was identified, in the early nineties when I began, as one of the three largest queer communities in the world. Amsterdam and San Francisco were the others. I've learned a thing or two; I'd say I've probably unlearned even more.

Introduction

When I started working on this book, I thought I'd offer an anecdote or two, then slide straight into a clear, concise presentation of the theological "argument" that's at its core. The more I wrote the more I realized it needed to be rooted in a story. My own story. Since it involves what is often identified as *the* hot-button issue of our time for the church, some readers will no doubt delight in picking that argument apart, getting up in arms about it, and in time-honored tradition, slagging the author. It won't be hard to do. I fully expect that sort of response to come from both "sides" and frankly I don't care much. (And really, racism, greed, addiction to power, and many other evidences of the church's abandonment of the gospel of the just kingdom of God should probably be closer to the top of the hot-button list.)

I do care about the other kinds of readers. I hope there will be queer folk who read this and will find in it both comfort and challenge. I hope some readers will be straight folk who, like me, are deeply convinced that the Bible is God's word, and as such can't just dismiss or ignore any part of it. Those readers want to really love, the way Jesus said we should; specifically, they want to really love queer people they've come to know and care about—and yet they find, sometimes, that their convictions about what the Bible teaches makes it hard to do so truly and fully. They sense that if ordinary people can seemingly be more accepting and more inclusive than God, we have a theological problem. I hope those good folk will find a way forward herein. Some other readers, I suspect, will be ones who have at some point decided that the Bible is just goofy or out of date about some issues, and can't really be taken seriously. They've simply ditched the passages that bother them and focus on the stuff that they think makes good sense. My hope for them is that this story will recover their confidence that the Holy Spirit breathes throughout the entire Bible and even reveal that the God depicted within it is good beyond what they've been able to imagine. Because he is, you know.

A word about the term "queer," which I use as a convenience throughout: there are lots of people within the LGTBQ2+ spectrum who don't like it. I don't blame them. (A few don't even like

LGTBQ2+.) However, I've been unable to find a better simple catch-all word to encompass people who identify as gay, lesbian, bisexual, transgender, asexual, two-spirited, nonbinary, or one of a slew of other terms that seem to keep proliferating. If the word bothers you, I apologize, and hope you might be able to receive it in the spirit of the King James Version phrase "a peculiar people." It's used in Deuteronomy (twice), Titus, and 1 Peter to describe people God has chosen as his own. I should note too that, for the sake of simplicity, my story only directly references gay, lesbian, and trans people, although the ideas presented certainly cover the entire spectrum of sexual and gender identity.

You may realize that I frequently and inaccurately conflate transgender and same-gender attracted (gay, lesbian, and bi) people, at least by implication. I freely acknowledge that they are, quite evidently, not the same. The one group is identified by gender, the other by sexuality. It's worth noting that the sexual orientation of transgender people doesn't change after they've transitioned. I've conflated them (along with people who identify in a myriad of other ways along the LGTBQ2+ continuum) because gender and sexual identity are connected closely enough that the same general theological questions tend to arise about both, and it seems to me that many of the same biblical principles apply.

Since this is the story of an individual spiritual journey, not a theological treatise, I've not footnoted anything. I'm not trying to definitively "prove" anything. If it's really necessary, I've noted my source in the text. If you encounter a paragraph that makes you wonder, "Where on earth did he get that?" I'm sure the good folks at Google will make it plain. As I said, this is no scholarly work. I should also make it absolutely clear that I am not offering anything in this book as Sanctuary's "position" on any matter. (Sanctuary is the community and church I work and hang out in.)

All quotations are from the English Standard Version, unless otherwise noted.

Right then. I think that covers it. Make yourself comfortable and we'll get started.

1

"Well, I Use You, Don't I?"

BY THE TIME I met John over lunch, he had become both living legend and salacious rumor to me. That was in the spring of 1992, but I'd encountered him years before while still in my teens. He was the much-older boyfriend of a girl my older brothers used to hang out with up at the lake sometimes. The way I remember him, he'd had a mane of thick brown hair and a full beard, broad shoulders, and a deep tan. Jeremiah or Ezekiel in a swimsuit.

I probably talked to him a couple of times that summer, but I don't recall. He was a striking figure though, and I know I spoke to my mother about him. He was the director of a well-known evangelical Christian camp at the time, and a leader of church young people in general. Through the fall and winter months, he led an all-city worship gathering for them in a downtown church—ironically, the very church building that would much later become home to the Sanctuary community, where I have lived and breathed and had my being for close to thirty years now. I was surprised to find out that my mother had taught him Sunday School as a child; she spoke fondly of him, and with compassion about the difficult situation in which he had grown up: his father had died when John was just fourteen years old.

I must have said something about a guy in his thirties dating a girl who was barely twenty. My mother smiled a secret smile, watching John and his girl trying to throw each other off the neighbor's dock.

"Oh," she said, "he'll never marry her."

If I asked why, she didn't tell me.

But she was right. The relationship ended soon after that. I kept hearing about John now and then. I attended a few of those youth gatherings, and there was no denying that he had charisma by the boat load, but I was more interested in checking out the girls than I was in him, or anything he had to say. Through the next few years, the anecdotes about and references to John shifted from admiring, to concerned, to enigmatic. He was certainly all over the place, wasn't he? He seemed to be struggling some. He'd needed to back away, a little. Uh oh, he'd had a breakdown. . . . And the trickle of information stopped. John slipped from view, landed in a well-we-don't-talk-about-that limbo.

It was a long time until I next saw him, and he was on TV. It was a local talk show; John was savaging a conservative minister of some sort who was trying to articulate and defend what he considered to be biblical sexual values. John had lost much of his golden aura, and he'd gained a fiery anger. He was aggressively gay, razor sharp, and totally out there. Although he still identified as Christian, it wasn't a version of the faith that I recognized. That poor minister never had a chance.

Several years later, I discovered that a friend of mine had shared a house with John and two or three other young men while he was going to university. At the time, none of them had known what was bothering John, but it shook them severely to watch the man they'd looked up to descend into anxiety, depression and, finally, a full-blown nervous breakdown. None of the church leaders who had built him up, my friend said, had ever come around to check on him. My guess is that they knew what John's struggle was really about—he probably told them—and they had no idea how to deal with it. John had become untouchable.

The crazy, extreme behaviors of the ghettoized gay community in the 1980s were the kind of thing that Christians, and to be fair, many others, either whispered about in a horror that was tinted with no small measure of gleeful titillation or tried to describe soberly and clinically as a means of proving just how aberrant these debauched specimens of humanity were. Rumor had it that John had dived into it all head first. And, think of all those young boys and young men he had had access to! How many must he have interfered with? It may seem ridiculous and offensive to make that kind of leap now, but it didn't then—not to straight folks. The common assumption, and not just in the church but in society at large, was that all queer folk had abandoned any sort of morality at all and were sexually insatiable.

Nobody ever came forward with an accusation. The friend of mine who had lived with him told me that, to his knowledge, John had never even confided the nature of his struggle to the young men who lived in his house, much less tried to seduce them. Not long after my lunch with John, I would begin to hear repeatedly from volunteers and staff of the AIDS Committee of Toronto—never from John himself—that he had been a hero in the gay community during the early years of the AIDS crisis in the mid- to late eighties. During that horrifying era, as a licensed funeral director, he prepared for burial all the bodies of the men who succumbed to the disease that was scything through the gay community in the city of Toronto, as it was around the world. No other undertaker would touch them.

Many years later, John would tell me that it was in fact his Christian faith that remained a singular light in the deep darkness of his journey toward accepting himself as a gay man. It was a Christian community in Boston that brought him back from the brink and stood him on his feet. And stand he did; in the maelstrom of death and despair that was the AIDS-afflicted gay community in Toronto of the eighties and early nineties, John's faith anchored him as he not only prepared the bodies of gay men for burial, but often officiated at their funerals. He'd gone back to school and, in 1989, was ordained a minister in a mainline denomination.

When I met him for that first lunch, I hadn't seen him for probably sixteen or seventeen years, not since that summer at the lake. I had just begun hanging out on the streets in the downtown core of Toronto—I called it "doing outreach" when pressed by church folks to give account for my activities; it was a practice that would soon give birth to a little foundling community of homeless people, addicts, prostitutes, street rounders, and a handful of earnest young Christians, which we would call Sanctuary. John had been an associate at a nearby church for a few years at that point. Apart from his normal liturgical and pastoral duties, he'd established a men's hostel in the church (a sprawling old pile) and was on the cusp of founding a bereavement support center. There couldn't have been many people better qualified for such an endeavor. He'd buried hundreds, many of them friends, during the AIDS epidemic which, in 1992, was still picking up speed.

Despite our tenuous connection, and knowing that I came from the same firmly fundamentalist tradition and convictions that had rejected him, John agreed readily to meet. The hair and beard had been trimmed and tamed, salt-and-peppered with the years. He was still lean and fit, and he wore a beautifully cut gray suit. Blue eyes danced beneath dark eyebrows. But for the black shirt and parson's collar, he'd have looked at home sliding out of the driver's seat of a Porsche, or behind the wheel of a yacht in one of those early retirement ads.

I remember little of what we discussed, although there must have been some catching up on the current circumstances of mutual acquaintances, and descriptions of what our own ministry lives looked like. I know he mentioned his partner of, I think, six or seven years. Interesting, that, since his denomination at the time did not affirm "practicing" gay or lesbian people in ministry, and had, in fact, defrocked another man who had, not long before, come out to his congregation and introduced his life partner. This was 1992, remember, when almost no churches or even secular social organizations were affirming same-gender relationships (I certainly wasn't), and legal marriage was a distant, not very realistic dream for gay and lesbian couples.

John had a plummy, radio announcer's voice, too, so he could afford to speak in a low, confidential tone. But it wasn't his vocal quality or the cut of his suit that drew me to him. Something happened across that table, and I know it happened for John too, as we talked about it later.

It was as if the usual curtain of propriety and caution that hangs between mere acquaintances had been drawn swiftly aside. Both of us had sat down expecting to be superficially friendly, civil—and careful. We knew what each other represented, or so we thought, and imagined ourselves to be on opposite sides of a great divide. I'm not sure what motivated John to accept my invitation, but I had extended it because I realized that my newly adopted neighborhood included not only street people, but also one of the world's largest gay and lesbian communities. (Kids, this was so long ago that the term LGBTQ had yet to be invented, let alone 2+.) In my naive enthusiasm to announce the gospel of Jesus Christ, I imagined that it was up to me to shine his light into a dark place. I suppose I expected to find in John a jaded, defensive soul with a cynical overlay of official but empty religion.

Instead, it felt like I was talking to someone I had known intimately all my life. John was possessed of a deep, obvious spirituality of the kind that has gone through the fire and come out refined, luminous. His compassion for struggling people of every stripe, not just queer folk, was clear. He loved God. His life was announcing the good news every day, in both word and deed. Jesus was his Savior, and his Lord. I knew these things about John, not just because he said them, but because everything about him carried the unmistakable, unfakeable whiff of eternity. I knew because something in my own soul confirmed it.

I saw John now and then over the next ten years, and although we maintained a good friendship, I never again felt that connection with quite the same intensity. It was as if, that day, the Spirit had sat at the table with us, sharpening our vision and hearing, opening our hearts, interpreting for us things that words alone can never truly communicate.

I left the restaurant badly rattled.

By the time my feet hit the sidewalk, the lovely sense of sitting before a crackling fire with God and a dear friend was gone. My mind reeled with question after question as I walked back to Sanctuary.

How could this be? John was homosexual, and not just by inclination, but by lifestyle. And yet, he was doing really good ministry, real Jesus stuff. I had been raised in a "closed" Brethren assembly, and while there are a number of points on which I would now disagree with the doctrine of such churches, they had at least one great characteristic: they produced an extraordinarily high level of biblical literacy among their congregants. The passages that prohibit or comment adversely on same-gender sexual activity raced through my mind, and beneath them rumbled the assumptions of my culture and training.

It was wrong, no question—wrong, wrong, wrong!—and yet God was nevertheless clearly "using" John. The very idea of being "used" by God, as if we are to him merely instruments to be picked up and put down according to need, is one I find demeaning to both God and humanity now. But that's how I thought at the time, and it seemed clear to me that John was no fit vessel for God's service.

Objection after objection plowed through my thoughts and shaped themselves into a stream-of-consciousness prayer of complaint and puzzlement. I felt betrayed, sucked in by a spiritual shell game.

"But-but-but . . ." I sputtered like an old one-lung motor. "How could you use *him*?"

Eventually I ran out of gas. Into my bewildered, disoriented mind slipped a thought, and it rang like the voice of God.

"Well, I 'use' *you*, don't I?"

2

That Gently Diverging Course

LISTEN, I DON'T THINK I was any more homophobic than was common at that time. In fact, I don't think I was really homophobic, per se, at all, in the sense of being afraid of or repulsed by queer folk. I hadn't had that much conscious contact with queer people, but I'd certainly had some. The concept of "coming out of the closet," now almost a colloquial relic, wasn't even a thing yet when I was a teenager: I never had a single avowedly queer school mate, although I'm positive some "came out" later. I'm sure it doesn't feel like it to my queer friends even now, but the relative speed with which "alternative sexualities" have become accepted in the mainstream, after centuries of being kept hidden or on the margins, is astonishing.

I had two obviously gay teachers in high school—a school that, in the mid-1970s, was rife with homophobia—and while I could barely tolerate one, I quite liked the other. Mr. King, the librarian, was prissy and officious, and nobody could stand him. Inevitably, he was referred to as Mr. Queen, often to his face, and routinely tormented by the older male students. I remember a mob of senior boys barricading him into a study room with a stack of carrel desks, while he pounded the door with his mustache quivering and his face a bright scarlet. Vicious treatment for a man who was, at worst, vaguely annoying to some. It was also, I admit with shame, enormously amusing at the time.

Mark Topham, one of the art teachers, was more flamboyant by far. He would pirouette around the room, his long black mop flying, and gush over the work of the more talented students. (Not mine, alas.) He'd perch on the corner of his own desk, or one of ours, with one knee over the other and his long-fingered hands fluttering, chuckling over some little witticism. Marky, we called him. Like I said, for whatever reason I liked the man. He was happy, at ease with himself, in a way that Mr. King didn't appear to be. Maybe it was as simple as that.

Later, when I went to university, I spent most of my spare time hanging out in the coffee shop that was home turf to students in the dance faculty. The girls were fabulous, and many of the boys, perhaps because the school boasted a large, loud "Homophile Association," seemed bent on being more feminine than the girls.

The thing is, none of that ever really bothered me. I heard lots of my male peers talk about how repugnant they found the very thought of man-on-man sex (strangely, they didn't seem to feel the same about girl-on-girl), but it never struck me as particularly icky or outrageous, just foreign. Let's face it, there's something absurd and vaguely humorous about the mechanics of any consensual sexual encounter.

No, I didn't have deep visceral reactions to homosexuality. I just thought it was morally, biblically wrong, like robbing a convenience store. Probably, because whatever we say, Christians do tend to rank sin, and illicit sex is at the top of the list, I thought it was more serious than that.

That little inner voice—"Well, I 'use' you, don't I?"—challenged my sense of personal moral superiority, and adjusted my course by a degree or two. That doesn't sound like much, and it wasn't at first, but any sailor or pilot can tell you that a tiny directional change maintained over a long journey will deliver you to a radically different destination. At the time, it only made me aware of my need to practice a little humility and increased my gratitude for the grace of God I still so often take for granted.

But it didn't answer my fundamental problem. I had been taught the Scripture from the time I was old enough to learn anything, and I'd been blessed with a literary bent that helped me retain much of what I learned. I had accrued a deeply rooted conviction, which abides to this day, that the Bible is the word of God, and as such, to be trusted utterly. I'd studied it avidly, for hours each week over more than a decade past, routinely going back to the Greek or Hebrew to unlock passages a verse at a time, a word at a time. I had inherited a strong hermeneutical ethic; I knew the stories intimately; on almost any given subject, I could quote the applicable references and offer an interpretation. (Whether accurate or not is another matter.) I *loved* the Bible then, and I love it more now.

Everything I knew told me that John's "lifestyle choices," as we tended to euphemize sexuality at the time, placed him beyond the pale of Christian praxis. So, okay, grace. Fine, I had nothing to brag about morally either. But wasn't he deliberately, repeatedly, and without repentance engaging in sinful behavior? On the other hand, he clearly loved God and sought to serve him, and, on the evidence, God was returning the favor.

It might not have been the first time, and it wouldn't be the last, that I found my theology didn't work the way it was supposed to. It was, I think, the first time I was ever forced to actually face that reality and wrestle with the problem, instead of ignoring it or explaining it away in some convenient fashion.

Turns out I would sail that gently diverging course for a long, long time, battling confusing swells and contrary winds the whole way. It would be twenty years before I'd find a place where I dared to drop anchor.

Sitting in the circle of volunteers-in-training, I dreaded the moment when it would be my turn to introduce myself. Around we went, twenty or so, perched on stackable chairs in a meeting room of the AIDS Committee of Toronto. One after another, they declared themselves: men who had just been diagnosed with HIV (murmurs of sympathy), or had lost a partner or friends to the disease (deep nods of recognition); lesbian women who were probably safer from AIDS than anyone in the city, but whose circle of friends was being decimated (broad smiles of appreciation); a straight woman or two of a certain age, whose sons were already gone, or were deep in the fight (smiles broader still).

One of these things, I thought to myself, is not like the others.

"Hi, my name is Greg," I started out, when it came my turn. Deep breath. "And I'm straight. But it's not my fault—I was born that way."

A moment of stunned silence, then a gale of laughter.

"Don't worry, honey," one of the men called out. "You're safe here!"

I breathed out and smiled my own appreciation.

"Also, I'm married. To a woman."

"Eeew, gross!"

"Baby, it doesn't matter—I was married to a girl once too! You can get over it!"

"I have kids, four of them."

"Oh no, a breeder!"

"And, um . . . I'm an evangelical pastor."

Dead silence. It might have been my imagination, but I thought a couple of them pushed their chairs back. Betty Ann, the volunteer coordinator, knew this about me already. She smiled at me from across the circle. Years later, she would admit that, from the moment she received my application, she assumed she would have to tell me sooner, probably, or possibly later that I wasn't a suitable volunteer candidate. I think that, at that moment, she was waiting for me to blow myself up. There was no laughter this time.

"I'm here because I know I look like the enemy. I know people like me have hurt people like you a lot, for a long time. I want to help hurting people in my neighborhood, and I know I need to learn how from you. So I don't hurt anyone else."

Most churches could learn a lot from that group about how to receive the stranger, extend grace, and be courageously vulnerable. During my six-year tenure with ACT, I never encountered another straight male volunteer, and I know for sure I was the only evangelical pastor. But I never felt less than welcomed, valued, and affirmed. Betty Ann would, within about a year, begin to invite me to address every new volunteer intake group. In a couple of scenarios, I was even trusted, and honored, to be a spokesperson for ACT volunteers.

My lunch meeting with John had been, in part, responsible for my decision to offer myself as a volunteer in an organization run by and for queer people. Although I was unable to untangle the theological knot into which he had tied me, I realized that I needed to learn more, and to do so in an environment that challenged rather than confirmed my convictions.

I should point out here that it wasn't only, or even primarily, the queer community that was revealing the cracks in my foundation. Already, in those early days, I was discovering that the street-involved people who occupied the majority of my focus did not respond to the gospel, as I understood it, as they were supposed to.

"If any man be in Christ, he is a new creature," I had learned (1 Cor 5:17; yes, the King James Version). "Old things are passed away; behold, all things are become new."

I suppose I had thought—was encouraged to think—that new life in Christ was essentially binary in its effect. Put your trust in Jesus, and automatically a spiritual switch was flipped, turning off the old sinful stuff and turning on the new godly desires. Silly, I know, but it's still what gets taught by inference and expectation, if not explicitly, in a lot of places. If I'd paid any attention at all to my own moral struggles and how they lingered, how little and slowly they changed, how often I slipped back into old habits, I might have been less surprised.

I was watching lifelong addicts, victims of horrifying childhood abuse, and people suffering from mental illnesses plead repeatedly with God for deliverance, often in tears. There was no question some believed that they were guilty sinners—almost all seemed to believe that, even if they were atheists—and God's grace through Christ was their only hope. But healing and real change, if it came at all, came for the most part so incrementally that it could hardly be marked.

Later, I would look back over long years and be astonished at the enduring faith some of those men and women displayed, and the depth of healing they experienced over time. Usually, that healing looked nothing like I would have expected it to. Those men and women became true heroes of faith to me. There's no doubt in my mind that their faith far exceeds my own; their transformation is greater than anything I have experienced within myself. They have been better teachers of the nature of true faith than any pastor, preacher, or professor I've ever encountered.

Strangely, the dismantling of my theological expectations, my neat propositional gospel with its presumed rules and predictable outcomes—the measurables of my faith—led me back to the Jesus who lives so vibrantly in the gospels. If I couldn't heal the lepers and the lame as he did, I at least wanted to walk among them with him.

That kind of thinking would land me in some odd places.

3

Disorientation

"Excuse me," I said to the pretty little Asian woman, touching her shoulder gently to get her attention. "Forgive me if I'm being too forward, but may I ask—what are you doing here?"

She was more than pretty, truth be told. She must have been all of five feet tall once she stepped out of the spike heels, with long glossy black hair and a complexion the color of honey. Although she was so tiny, she had the proportions of a pin-up girl, and most of it was on display, sheathed only in an outfit that called Wonder Woman to mind. Almond eyes and impossibly long lashes.

And she was standing in Bar 501, the closest thing the gay village had then to a neighborhood pub. Other bars on Church Street hosted most of the beautiful young male bods; denizens of the 501 referred to those as meat markets, and prided themselves on being the more down-to-earth, rough and tumble crowd. In the early nineties, Church Street was still often referred to as the "gay ghetto"—it truly wasn't safe to be openly gay and wander around outside its borders, especially at night. The "out" queer population was densely concentrated in that neighborhood in large part for the security numbers offered. But there were ghettos within the ghetto too: the dark bars with blacked out windows where older, still-closeted men cruised young boys, many of them street youth; the leather bars; the bath houses; at the top of the heap, the meat markets; and lesbian bars. There wasn't much gay/lesbian social crossover then. The women drank and partied with women, and the men with men.

I used to go to the 501 every couple of weeks with an outreach partner or two and shoot pool during the day. On our late-night street walks, we'd usually stop by on our way home, as we had this time, to chat a bit with friends we'd made. I'd never seen the pretty little Asian woman there before.

She didn't seem entirely put off by my approach, but she did look puzzled.

"What do you mean?" she said.

"Well, look around," I responded, indicating the bar full of men dressed mostly in jeans and work shirts or tank tops. "Apart from Diane over there behind the bar, I think you're the only woman in the place. And you look like you should be on a TV show."

It was a version, I guess, of "What's a sweet young thing like you doing in a dump like this?" If she hadn't assumed I was gay like almost everyone else in the place, she'd probably have thought I was hitting on her. I swear I wasn't, but she certainly stood out in that crowd. She laughed quietly and splayed a slender hand demurely over her décolletage.

Then she leaned close and, in what passed for a whisper amidst the clamor of the bar, she said, "I'm here because I'm a boy, silly."

I gaped foolishly, and she laughed again.

I'd met a number of other trans women, almost always out "on the stroll," a couple of blocks of dimly lit street where they sashayed back and forth waiting for a car to stop. I'd never been so completely taken in.

Cassandra, like many other trans women at the time, had come to Toronto from Southeast Asia because the Clarke Institute of Psychiatry had one of the most progressive gender transition programs in the world, coupled with a large and (more or less) accepting queer community. Once here, she needed money for treatment, but finding legitimate work when her documents said she was male, and she looked like a woman, was impossible. It's also likely that, as she was in Canada for medical treatment, she lacked a work visa. She'd had the hormone treatments and breast implants and was completing the required time living as a woman before she would qualify for the final, irrevocable genital surgeries. In the meantime, she too was working the streets.

Disorientation is often a necessary part of the process of reorientation. Cassandra's entire person and experience left me spinning again. I'd come to the point where I felt like I could, at least in some remote intellectual fashion, understand men being attracted to men and women to women. I certainly understood the attraction of men to the actual women I'd met on some of the other strolls. The dark call of anonymous, totally selfish sex with a carica- ture of femaleness, a woman whose true identity and personhood was of no consequence in the transaction, and who existed in the moment only to serve *me! me! me!* was one I'd had to resist myself. Those dark urges, the voice hissing within, "You could do this, and no one would ever know . . ." led me to take measures to ensure that I'd never be alone in a situation where I might be tempted to respond. It also helped, no doubt, that I had very little money.

Maybe that voice came from the pit, or maybe from my own wounded spirit. Even so, it was also the word of God, "sharper than any double-edged sword, piercing to division of soul and of spirit, of joints and of marrow; and discerning the thoughts and intentions of the heart" (Heb 4:12). It was a kind of spiritual sur- gery. He was laying me open, showing me what really festered deep within, and it shook me.

Although I "understood" same-gender sex and could identify with some of the more twisted attractions of hetero sex, the con- cept of men wanting other men who looked like women remained one too many hairpin curves on the road for me. (Most of the johns that cruised the stroll where Cassandra had worked knew exactly what they were looking for.) Still does. But I was beginning to see that I didn't need to understand; that, in fact, "understand- ing" might be a euphemism for judging. The plank in my own eye left me poorly equipped for removing the speck of dust from someone else's.

That doesn't mean that I now thought it was okay. I didn't. It did mean that I was beginning to realize how little I understood about the "problem" of queer sexual and gender identities and experience. And most importantly, it left me ruminating on the possibility that my own sexual self was no more or less essentially broken than those of my queer friends.

A theology that doesn't work in the real world, in real time, is no theology at all. The biblical concept of righteousness is, in concise terms, God's justice lived in the context of human relationships. It's not an abstract concept, but a praxis one—it must be applied to be real, to be true and right and good. Paul taught us, I knew, that the essential function of the law was to prove to us that we couldn't keep it, so that we would come to understand that faith in God's grace was our only hope (Rom 7:7ff.; Gal 3:10ff.).

I could no longer believe that this God of grace would set rules that John, Cassandra or all those men in the ghetto were simply unable to follow, and then condemn them for the failure. The God I thought I had known did set rules, but also guaranteed that, once saved, everyone would be able to follow them. *It didn't work.* God was slipping the leash I'd had him on. Grace must be the answer, but how did it work? Surely it wouldn't simply set aside the teachings of Scripture—God would never say, "Hey, all that stuff I told you? Never mind. Just foolin." It couldn't be a matter of him saying, in effect, "Eew, that's disgusting. But I guess I'll just hold my nose and forgive you anyway." Could it? Shouldn't redemption—not just forgiveness, but a glorious remaking—extend, somehow, to this too?

If I'd thought about it much at all, I had thought that addressing homosexuality or those other messy problems in one's life, like addiction, mental illness, abuse traumas, and so on, was simply a matter of will or submission or prayer or some such. I had thought it was a matter of behaviors, or choice, rather than identity. I was learning differently.

For who on earth would willingly choose Cassandra's path? Who would take on those kinds of burdens just for grins, or to be rebellious, or whatever lame constructs my training had inculcated in me? How could I even begin to understand what she'd gone through to get where she was? Who would go through the agonies and loss John had endured as a young man if there was another, easier, more apparently honorable path?

I remembered the man I had literally picked up off the sidewalk not long before. Walking up Yonge Street, Toronto's main street, which passes by Sanctuary less than a block away, I'd seen a body crumpled on the concrete below the wide window alcove of an art gallery. It was around midnight, and I assumed it was probably one of my homeless friends, drunk and passed out for the night. I crossed the street just to make sure he or she was alright. Getting a little closer, I could see the body moving a little, as if struggling to get up. He staggered to his feet, walking his hands up the window. It wasn't anybody I knew, and he wore the tight short shorts and sleeveless singlet that only gay men then favored. He stumbled a step or two and fell again.

It was dangerous for him to be there on Yonge Street alone at night. He was outside the "ghetto." There could be any number of boneheads tooling up and down the main drag looking for someone to hate on.

I had thought he was only drunk; it turned out my fears for him were entirely justified. While he definitely had been drinking—I could smell it, and it was probably why he had wandered outside the safe zone—the real issue was that he'd already been badly beaten. His nose looked like someone had attacked it with a potato masher. His eyes were swollen almost shut, his head and torso were smeared all over with blood. He was barely conscious.

"Steve," he answered me through split lips, lisping blood, on the third try.

By the way he moved as I helped him to his feet, I was pretty sure Steve would find some boot-shaped bruises on his torso in the morning, and maybe some broken ribs. He was unable to walk alone. I stuck my shoulder in his armpit, dragged his arm across my own shoulders and held it there by the wrist. It took a while to get him the few blocks to Sanctuary, where my car was parked, and another major effort to get him out of the car again and into the entrance vestibule of his apartment.

There, some vestige of self-preserving instinct returned, and he insisted on entering alone. I backed off but stayed to watch. He made it through the locked doors and collapsed onto a couch in the foyer.

Some months afterward, I bumped into Steve on the street. He claimed not to recognize me, which might have been true, and insisted that no, he'd never been jumped on the street. But his darting-eyed embarrassment said otherwise.

Only a few months after I first met her at Bar 501, Cassandra was beaten to death by a john, presumably someone who had been "fooled" as I had, until they really got down to business. I found out via a brief paragraph buried in the middle pages of the newspaper. It was only the first of several such murders of queer acquaintances and people I'd come to know as friends that I would experience in the next few years. It put a fine point on my growing conviction that sexual orientation and gender identity afforded most people little room for choice.

Cassandra hadn't been trying to fool anyone. Not me, and not that john. Not herself, and certainly not God. She'd just been trying to become who she believed herself to be.

I thought of the dozens of men I'd met on the Steps, a broad set of shallow stairs in front of a coffee shop that had become a Mecca for the international gay community. Gay men gathered there at all times of day, but especially late at night. It was a regular stop on my Thursday night route. I'd buy a coffee and stand there talking with the other hangers-out. After a while, it was generally known that I was straight and a Christian—and, fortunately, that I was safe.

Some of those men began to tell me a little of their own stories and struggles on those soft summer nights after the bars had closed. They'd tell me how their families had written them off and try to laugh about it. They'd talk about how hard it was to get and keep a job unless you pretended to be straight—a situation in those days so endemic that it surprised me not in the least. More than a few had married women, and even fathered children, either to try to convince themselves they were straight, or to provide a cover for what they desperately hoped could be normal lives.

A surprising number talked about how they'd been Christians, until they couldn't any longer deny to themselves that they were gay. As far as they were concerned, they simply couldn't be both gay and Christian, and they couldn't not be gay. It's not that they didn't want to be Christian. They didn't stop believing in God or Jesus and the Bible.

On the contrary. What remained of their faith simply ratified what others had told them: they were damned by a God who was disgusted with them. And *they were unable to do anything about it.* Many had tried "therapies" of one kind or another, often under the auspices of Christian organizations, only to find that they changed nothing. They talked about knowing as young as five or six years old that they were different than other boys, and the later conviction that this simply meant they had been condemned from birth. They'd desperately wanted to be normal. They'd tried prayer, submitted themselves to deliverance ministries, attended Bible studies and support groups and even shock therapy geared to eradicating their sinful inclinations. They pled with God for miracles, but nothing happened. Somehow, they were beyond the scope of his grace. Their despair and self-loathing was heartrending.

Thankfully, at least some of these societal dispositions, in some places, have changed in the intervening years. But the enormous cost these men paid so unwillingly persuaded me there was little choice involved. If they could not choose, and God would seemingly not "heal" them, how were they supposed to live? How then did God view them? What did redemption look like in their lives? What kind of gospel could I, in my ignorance and confusion, hope to announce to them? For that matter, if, as I was beginning to suspect, my own case was really no better, what hope did the gospel I had been preaching hold for me?

4

Even If It Leaves Me Limping

IF JOHN, CASSANDRA, AND the men on the Steps had set my neatly ordered theological world tumbling, Roxanne would dump it upside down and shake the change from its pockets. She was the focus of my first assignment as a newly graduated volunteer of the AIDS Committee of Toronto. Betty Ann, the volunteer coordinator, was more than a little surprised that I hadn't washed out during training, as were a few others, I'm sure. For me, the deeper I got into it, the more it made sense. "Incarnational ministry" as a concept had yet to arrive among evangelical churches—they were typically going on about "friendship evangelism," which, as far as I could tell, meant being friendly with unsaved people until they let their guard down, and you could sock them with the good news that they were lost and on their way to hell— but I was rediscovering the Jesus of the gospels.

Maybe, in fact, I was actually discovering him for the first time. The dispensationalist teaching of my youth essentially gutted the gospels by asserting that all kingdom teaching was for a future time, when Christ would rule on earth. I had yet to fully work my way through that morass, but just observing where Jesus went, who he connected with, and what he said and did was fresh, freeing, and so very different from the rigorous doctrinal structures I'd grown up with. Those doctrines were rooted almost exclusively in the letters of Paul, and I was beginning to realize that, rather than interpreting his teaching in the light of the teaching and life of Jesus, we had been doing the reverse. Paul, I had begun to suspect, would be shocked.

Because of my encounters in the Sanctuary neighborhood, the gospels were, for the first time, making sense to me. They were a coherent whole, instead of illustrative snippets from the life, death, and resurrection of our Savior. I had trusted a high and holy Jesus as my savior when I was just a child but now I was falling in love with the incredible, beautiful person I encountered in the gospel stories, too. As deeply moved as I was by the agonized, bleeding figure on the cross, and the glorious one bursting from the grave, I was discovering that he was even more. Savior and Lord, yes, but also Teacher, Master, and Friend. Honoring him as all that didn't just, or even primarily, mean submitting to church doctrines. It meant *following* him. Going to the kinds of places he went; hanging out with the kinds of people he hung out with; doing, to the best of my admittedly puny ability, the kinds of things that he did.

I was confused and full of unanswered questions, but I was having a great time.

More surprising even than my successful graduation from volunteer training was that Betty Ann gambled on sending me into a very sensitive situation right out of the chute. Roxanne was dying. As it would turn out, she was only a month or so from the end, and I would only get to be with her perhaps a dozen times.

My assignment was simple: be Roxanne's "buddy." In many cases, participating in the "Buddy Program" meant the volunteer functioned much like a personal assistant to the person with AIDS—doing some shopping for him, for instance, or laundry, or driving him somewhere. I say "him" because, at the time, women with HIV/AIDS were relatively rare. That alone made Roxanne intriguing. I couldn't wait to meet her.

She was long and cadaverously lean, with lank blond hair and eyes that seemed too large for her skull. The ghetto in the early nineties was rife with thin young men with similarly wasting faces, indentations just below their temples that were deep enough to fit your thumb into, their teeth a little too big for their mouths, tottering around on bony legs. I'd seen and even met quite a few of those men but being with Roxanne was the first time I'd really gotten close to someone with AIDS. I was seeing close up what those young men had to look forward to. Her flesh and muscle had melted away, rendering her a skeleton minimally padded, wrapped in parchment skin. Protease inhibitors were being posited hopefully but were still years away from being available. They would first radically slow the disease and, as they were refined, effectively render it a chronic but manageable condition for those who could afford them. But they would be far, far too late for Roxanne and thousands more. An HIV-positive diagnosis in the late eighties and well into the nineties generally meant a prognosis of anywhere between months and a few years.

She was in a hospital bed the entire time I knew her, which meant that there really wasn't anything for me to do for her, apart from occasionally fetching some water or tissues. I'd just go sit by her bed and we would talk, or not, as she was inclined. Her condition had caused some dementia, which was increased by copious pain meds, so she didn't always make sense and was often in and out of consciousness. She seemed to accept and welcome my presence immediately and was intrigued to hear about my family and work.

I wondered about how she had contracted the virus, but it was bad form to ask. I couldn't say why she didn't seem like an addict to me; sharing needles among intravenous drug users was then the most common source of infection among positive women. Maybe she was one of those who had received a transfusion of bad blood in the years before the Red Cross had known what to look for.

With trepidation, I asked after her family.

Oh, they were very supportive, Roxanne said. They visited all the time, called frequently, brought flowers. Very loving. She would introduce me when our visits coincided.

Eventually her story came out in scraps and phrases, rambling circuitous anecdotes delivered in the detached cadences of a mind drifting on a placid lake of morphine.

Roxanne had been born into what she said was a normal, loving middle-class suburban home. She was hermaphrodite, now more commonly called intersex: that little newborn baby had vestigial sexual organs of both genders and hormones levels smack in the middle of the male and female ratios. Having had four children of my own, I could only imagine how thoroughly aghast her parents must have been. Doctors told them there really wasn't much indication as to which gender would be preferable; the child's gender was as perfectly ambiguous as it was possible to be. Mum and Dad could flip a coin or make a choice for boy or girl. Either way, there was work to be done.

They chose boy. As he grew, little Rox (not his name then, obviously enough, but I never did find out what her birth name was) endured hormone therapies to deepen his voice and promote facial hair growth, and multiple genital surgeries to remove some bits and enhance or construct others. He tried hard to be a boy, a boy like his parents wanted. It didn't work very well. He didn't care for the sports others followed or played so avidly. He was self-conscious of his body, that his anatomy and its development were lacking, despite all the treatment and ongoing surgical tweaks.

Another part of the problem was that he was attracted to other boys. By his late teens he had left home and landed in the ghetto. He buried his uncertainty for a few years, submersing himself in what was at that time, by all accounts, a wild social and sexual scene. He found more acceptance there than he'd ever had before, and even met a small handful of people who had similar issues. Ultimately, Rox decided that he was, after all, a she.

Hormone treatments again, depilatory treatment this time to undo the effect of the previous hormone treatments, psychiatric support and assessment, the absurd years of living as a woman, who had been a man, who had been neither or both and was really a woman. Then the surgeries of her childhood, in reverse. And after all that, the news that she had tested positive.

I could not begin to imagine what it had been like to live any part of her life.

I never found out whether it was unprotected sex, IV drug use, or bad blood transfusions that infected her, but it hardly mattered. Infected she was. If you didn't know, hearing that someone was HIV *positive* would sound like a good thing, wouldn't it?

I walked into her hospital room one day to find the bed empty, fresh sheets stretched tight, the intravenous tree and other equipment gone. The over-the-bed table parked neatly in the corner. That peculiar stillness in the air.

Nobody ever contacted me about a funeral. Nobody seemed to know how to contact her family. Never, during any visit with her over that last month of her life, did I encounter anyone else sitting by her bedside. I never saw the flowers she said they brought, nor a card on her bedside table; the phone never rang. I would imagine her parents took the body and buried her as privately as possible.

Did they still call her by the name they'd given her at birth? Is that what they put on the headstone? Did they refer to her as "him"? Did they refer to her at all?

The thought that Roxanne had never had a chance haunted me. If God is judge, on what basis would he judge her? By what criteria? What possibility of justice or redemption had there been in her tragic, impossible life? What real choice had she ever had? The idea that maybe she was, so sad, just one of those who fall through the cracks was totally unacceptable. I was convinced that although fractures abound in creation and every human system, there were no cracks to fall through in God. Somehow, Roxanne had to fit in him. She must be as precious to him as anyone else. I couldn't see how he could be God otherwise. I still can't.

I know that for increasing numbers of people, especially younger people, including Christian young people, questions like these are simply irrelevant. Same gender relationships? Not an issue. Transgender people? Just the way it is. If the Bible says some stuff we don't like or don't understand, well . . . let's go on to something else.

It's not enough for me. It wasn't then and isn't now. I do trust that the Bible is the word of God, and it's because I do that I need to understand how what it says applies. I don't want to just ignore the inconvenient bits, and neither do I want to adopt strong convictions just for the sake of having them. I think that if I'm willing to face the difficult issues and wrestle with them, as opposed to either dismissing or slapping a quick, definitive interpretation on them, I'll find that I'm wrestling with the angel of the Lord, just like Jacob. I don't want to let go until he blesses me, even if it leaves me limping.

Jacob discovered that the God who was willing to roll in the dirt with him all night long was far bigger than he'd ever imagined. I've found the same. The more I wrestle, the bigger he gets. I suppose that's the blessing. Sometimes it feels like the dawn will never come.

I had no answers about Roxanne, but the memory of her was like the voice of one crying out in the wilderness to me, "Clear the path—the Lord is coming through."

5

Certainty Is No Friend to Faith

THERE COULD HARDLY BE a more accurate description of what was happening to me than what follows in Isaiah's prophecy of the cataclysm that would occur when the Messiah arrived: "Every valley shall be lifted up, and every mountain and hill be made low; the uneven ground shall become level, and the rough places a plain" (Isa 40:4).

It is, I know, the grossest individualizing of Scripture to apply it so personally, but there's no doubt that my own theological "landscape" was undergoing an earthquake that would register way up there on the Richter Scale. Mountains of doctrinal conviction shook and began to crumble; new uncertainties rose beneath my feet. Crevasses opened up and the perdition below threatened to swallow me up.

Okay, I realize that's a little purple. But it did kind of feel like that at times. The valleys were heaving, and the mountains were tumbling, but the ground beneath me had certainly not yet "become level." Having been raised with a dogmatic faith, every point of doctrine challenged by these and many other relationships felt like direct attacks on my own personhood. Even worse, it seemed to me that if I admitted my growing theological uncertainties, I would lose my certainty of who God was—I would lose my hold on God, and then where would I be?

Well, where I always was, of course: safe in God's grip. In time I would realize that it was God who was dismantling my certainties, precisely so that I would be free to trust him instead of them. Certainty is no friend to faith.

"Trust in the Lord with all your heart," Proverbs 3:5 says, "and *do not lean on your own understanding.*" I was beginning to learn that my certainties about God and what the Bible taught on a variety of subjects might mean that I was trusting my own intellectual capacity, not God.

Despite my fears that I would "lose" God, I began to find that, as I became less sure of whether or not I was right, the closer and more real he seemed. Amid the fog that began to shroud other beliefs, Jesus shone more and more brightly as the Son of the Living God, Redeemer of All Creation. Intimacy was replacing certainty. A creeping awareness of God's largeness began to overtake the constraints my dogma had placed on my assumptions about his character. I started to suspect that I had been placing my faith in boilerplate theological systems and doctrines, rather than in God himself; that the dogmas that were supposed to reveal God instead often obscured him; and, finally, that they were a mechanism by which I was attempting to control God, rather than submitting to him. God was slipping the leash I'd had him on.

This was all much bigger, of course, than just my struggles to understand how queer folk were supposed to fit in the gospel picture. As I've mentioned, my friends who were addicted, homeless, mentally ill, or subject to post-trauma issues also resisted slotting themselves into my neat schematics. Almost nothing in this ministry life was turning out the way I'd imagined it.

As a kid, I had always found that the most exhilarating ride down a snow-covered hill was to be had on the vehicle with the most minimal options for control. A sled with steerable runners made the trip so predictable. A toboggan was a little better, but you could still drag a hand out one side or the other to adjust a bit. But on one of those saucer-like discs, or a simple sheet of plastic—there was no telling what might happen! That's what it felt like now: thrilling, nerve-wracking, bruising at times, leaving me afraid of a total wipeout, and more than a little dizzy.

It was fabulous.

Given that parts kept flying off my theology like fenders off a car in a demolition derby, it seemed evident that there were only two possible explanations: either the Bible was full of bumpf or my understanding of some of it was. I had been sure of so much, but people and events—and maybe God himself—kept chipping away at the foundations I stood on until it seemed likely I would tip over. I wanted clarity from God; God wanted faith from me. Guess who won?

There are more than a few who have essentially said, "This system of beliefs is nonsense. There must be no God at all." But to me, God wasn't just an idea I was sure was right, as was the case with most of my other convictions—he was a daily, intimate reality in my life. Philosophers might describe this as a noetic awareness, or immanence, but to me it was and is simply the abiding sense that God is present. Right here, with me. In fact, in the midst of this long struggle, he just kept becoming more so.

I was beginning to learn two important things:

1. Faith (in the midst of doubt) makes me aware of God's nearness, while certainty keeps him at a distance.

2. When doctrine or theology doesn't actually work in the real world, or is counter to the infinitely loving, faithful, merciful character of the God of the Bible, there's a problem with the theology.

In other words, theology has to work in the real world in real time. That's called a "praxis" theology—one that develops from and/or is proven by experiencing it—and I would argue that if it ain't that, it ain't legit. All theology is a human attempt to understand and explain God. Just saying that out loud makes it perfectly clear that since we are all finite, bound by culture, experience, education, personality and so on, only the most arrogant and misguided can be sure they have it all right. Claiming to be fully objective doesn't work and isn't actually "right"—it's simply not possible for it to be true. It's ultimately just our sad attempt to put God in a box.

One thing I had long since learned experientially, and not just as a precept, was that I could count on hearing God's voice in Scripture. By that I mean that if I listened, God seemed to be speaking to me. Not usually specific direction, despite my frequent desire for it, or even explanation of how to understand what I read, but small revelations of God's love and grace; not infrequently, a challenge to some behavior or attitude of mine.

I've loved the Bible since I was a kid and have always read and thought lots about what it has to say. I'd had a passing familiarity with those "prohibitive passages," but I'd never really been motivated to study them closely before. At a cursory reading, which was all I had ever done, they seemed pretty clear: homosexual behavior was just wrong. The underlying reason for that judgment seemed to be that God had made male and female to function together sexually, not people of the same gender. As far as I could tell, while cross-dressing was also condemned, the Bible had nothing at all to say to people who identified as transgender.

There are five passages in the Bible that comment explicitly on same-gender sexual activity: two in the Old Testament and three in the New. And of course, there's the famous Sodom and Gomorrah story in Genesis 19 in which the male residents of Sodom wanted to rape some visiting men; the two towns were destroyed by God. I went back to these passages to see if there was something I had missed.

If you're expecting some brilliant new exegesis of them, you'll be sadly disappointed. I have nothing new to add to the volume of commentary that's already been written on both sides of the issue. Just lots of questions and, maybe, a different perspective on how they fit in the biblical story as a whole.

I found that Leviticus and Paul were still saying the same things, and at least superficially those things were pretty clear.

Leviticus 18:22, 20:13: "Any man who has sex with a man should be put to death." That's about as direct as it's possible to be.

Paul was less blunt, but in Romans 1:26, 27, still clearly described women and men exchanging natural relations with each other for relations with those of the same gender as a symptom their abandonment of God. (If you want a truly scholarly and thought-provoking exegesis of this passage, read *Romans Disarmed*, by Sylvia Keesmaat and Brian Walsh, especially chapter 9; Brazos, 2019.) Then in 1 Corinthians 6:9 and 1 Timothy 1:10 he includes "effeminates" (or, "softies"; males who submit themselves to sexual use by other males) and "bed-men" (literally rendered; it means males who use other males sexually) in lists of those who won't enter the kingdom of God, "the lawless and disobedient." "Tops and bottoms," in the common parlance. "Pitchers and catchers."

And yet, questions arose for me. Why did Leviticus legislate so forcefully in the instance of gay sex, and, like Paul writing to the Corinthians and Timothy, say nothing at all about lesbians? Why did this prohibition seem so important to me (and many other Christians) when so many of the dictums of the law were so easily dispensed with? How could I be sure this one still mattered? Why did Jesus seemingly say nothing about it?

How did "exchanging natural relations" apply when most of the gay and lesbian people I knew claimed they knew they were different from the time they were children—many even before they hit puberty? What of people like my friend John who, in spite of their orientation, were still seeking God? Was "God giving them up to a debased mind" too? I knew people who had submitted to every so-called therapy they could find, in a fruitless effort to change. Hadn't God promised that whoever sought him would find him? The rest of that passage didn't seem to follow, either: the people I knew weren't full of evil, murder, or maliciousness, nor were most haters of God. Why had Paul included this apparently very serious stuff with low-grade evil-doing like being "insolent," "disobedient to parents," or just "foolish"? He was certainly adamant enough: he wrote that "those who practice such things deserve to die" (Rom 1:28–32).

Why did he differentiate between "effeminates" and "bed-men" in his comments to the Corinthians if the issue was simply man-on-man sex? ("Effeminate," or "soft," which he uses only in 1 Corinthians 6:9, and "man who beds" are literal translations of the Greek words he uses. Most versions imprecisely use more generic terms like "homosexuality," "men who have sex with men," or "men who practice homosexuality," which skews their meaning.)

Why was the prophet Ezekiel's interpretation of the reason for the destruction of Sodom and Gomorrah so different than what I had always been taught? The Lord's declaration is,

> Behold, this was the guilt of your sister Sodom: she and her daughters had pride, excess of food, and prosperous ease, but did not aid the poor and needy. They were haughty and did an abomination before me. So I removed them, when I saw it. (Ezek 16:49, 50)

Even the word "abomination" there has no implicit sexual connotation. From the context, it seemed so obvious that God's judgment had to do with justice, not sexuality. The rape the men of Sodom wanted to enact on the angels who had come to take Lot to safety was not fundamentally a sexual act—rape never is; it was a means of dominating and utterly humiliating people they saw as vulnerable, or as enemies.

I wondered why, if it was such a big issue, did Jesus seemingly say absolutely nothing about it?

But the question that rang loudest was simply, "Why is this so wrong?"

Yes, it deviated from the created order related in the early chapters of Genesis, but didn't practically everything? It seemed arbitrary, much like the prohibitions against eating pork. My fundamentalist upbringing had conditioned me to obey the letter of what Scripture said, whether I understood it or not, but even I could see that my obedience was selective. I loved pork, and so did most of the Christians I knew. I could tell that the dietary restrictions of the law and its sexual prohibitions were of a different order, but why was one still in force and not the other? Other prohibitions, such as incest, adultery, theft, lying, or murder, seemed focused on harm done to others. How, exactly, was same-gender sexual relationship harmful, unless it was in a context like those that applied to hetero sex? Was it wrong simply because there was no societal allowance for same-gender marriage?

I have to say that, while some biblical scholars were able to explain in reasonably convincing fashion that these prohibitive passages should not be in force for us today, nobody seemed to make an equally convincing case for actually affirming same-gender sexual relationships. In other words, they could argue, "The Bible doesn't condemn it," but not, "The Bible says it's good." I found much of the queer commentary so specious that, to me, it weakened a proposed affirming theology—assumptions and even authoritative statements that, of course, David and Jonathan were gay lovers, as were the centurion and his slave, who Jesus healed, in Matthew 8:5–13 and Luke 7:1–10; that Paul was queer because he wasn't married; even that John and Jesus himself had something going on. These "arguments" seemed more transparently hopeful than substantive to me. The centurion and slave, culturally speaking, seemed the most likely candidates. Luke did use a phrase that indicated the slave was precious or dear to the centurion; a strangely tender expression for a master/slave relationship. But at best a responsible reader would be limited to the possibility, not a definitive conclusion. It seemed likely to me that Matthew and Luke's audiences would be primarily contemplating the head-scratching fact that Jesus extended grace to the pagan oppressor—a Roman soldier, present because he was part of an occupying force—not the nature of the relationship between the two.

I still wanted to be obedient, but I also wanted to understand. These were questions I'd never really had before. I realized I only had them now because the issues were no longer abstract: they affected, directly and deeply, individual people I was coming to love. How did this apply to John, who God had so evidently not abandoned? What could I have said to Roxanne, when she had no real options? Or Cassandra? What about those men on the Steps, whose deep-of-the-night desolation revealed their continuing hunger for a God they'd come to believe would never accept them as he had created them?

I was beginning to admit to myself that biblical arguments are usually only conclusive if you want them to be.

6

Badly Broken and Buried Deep

THAT INKLING WAS CONFIRMED when, frustrated by my own inability to get definitive answers, I turned to reading any and every biblical commentary I could find on same-gender sexuality, pro or con. I did this for years, until long after I stopped finding any new perspectives. I read and reread the same handful of arguments couched in different language behind different covers. Ultimately, it just wasn't helpful.

I'd read a "conservative" commentary, book, or article and think, "Well, I guess my original position was the right one." My heart would sink, because of the implications for my queer friends. Then I'd read a "liberal" one and think, "Of course! That makes so much sense!" But the next would undercut the one before, and on and on, round and round it went. As I've said, I'm not a scholar. What was I supposed to do, choose the opinion I liked best? Play a theological version of Pin-the-Tail-on-the-Donkey?

As time went on, in either case, I became more critical, finding the holes in arguments on both sides of the issue. Most people only read material that will confirm the position they already hold, but I had no real position anymore, just a longing to find answers that expressed the infinitely loving and gracious character of the God I depended upon myself and held out that same love and grace to people who seemed condemned from the outset. In spite of often outstanding scholarship on the part of the authors—far, far greater than I'd ever be able to muster myself—none of the commentary I read gave me a firm place to land.

Finally, I concluded that the prohibitive passages offered me no hope of a conclusion. To find any kind of answer, I'd have to set them aside and find another approach.

It didn't help that I began to hear rumors of discontent from some corners of my supporting constituency. "Greg doesn't preach repentance anymore," certain unverifiable sources were quoted as saying sniffily. "It's all social gospel."

It mystified me that they could possibly know what I was or wasn't "preaching," as those commentators were comfortably ensconced at a great remove in outer suburbia and never witnessed what I did or didn't do or say on any given day.

I presumed that what they meant by my not preaching repentance was that they assumed that I didn't go around telling people in my neighborhood the good news that they were dirty rotten sinners on the fast road to hell. "Social gospel," I supposed, indicated that I was instead just telling people to be good, to do good, and if they were good enough God would let them through the pearly gates in the end. As far as I could tell, they had reached these conclusions because it was becoming common knowledge that I was spending my time hanging out with street people, addicts, prostitutes, and—worst of all—*homosexuals!*

The reality was that repentance had never seemed like a more material, practical necessity in my own life, and in the lives of the folks I was beginning to think of as *my* people. To repent, biblically, doesn't mean to feel sorry for sinning. It means to stop, change your way of thinking and the direction you're headed.

It was so obvious that so many of my friends needed to do exactly that. A wide range of antisocial behaviors and the addictions that were most often the suppurating wounds left by early life trauma certainly required a change of thinking and direction if there was any hope of recovery. To me, they weren't hookers, drunks, and lunatics. They were, and are, my brothers and sisters. Many have sustained such damage that it's a testament to their courage and endurance that they're still standing. In this regard, I admire them immensely, and I know that many have a faith that far surpasses mine. And yet, after all these years, it's still not altogether clear to me which comes first, the repentance or the healing. For more than a few, it seems to me, at least a measure of healing is necessary to make possible that change of thinking and direction. And God, from my perspective, doesn't miraculously heal people nearly often enough.

As for me, God was apparently forcing me to rethink almost everything. In those early years—through the nineties—it seemed as if God was stripping away, one by one, many of the precepts I had considered foundations of my faith, and not just in matters of sexual orientation and gender identity. Everything was up for grabs; not only my theological convictions, but my confidence in my own person faced challenges at every turn.

I had never really thought much about my own sexuality—which is not to say I hadn't thought much about sex: like most younger men, it felt at times as if I thought about it constantly. That didn't seem strange to me. As far as I could tell, it was just the way guys were. I still think that's pretty accurate. Lust was dangerous and couldn't be given free reign, but you could indulge in a little here and there without much harm; it was normal.

When I started full-time, in March 1992, at what would before long become Sanctuary, I spent most of my time just hanging out on the streets. I walked the downtown core comprehensively and regularly, at all times of the day and night, as a means of getting to know my new turf and meeting the people who also hung out there—especially those who lived on the margins, in the alleys and shadows. It was a different world in the wee small hours, when the suits and tourists had gone home, and regular folk were in their beds.

The center of any large city is never really dark, not with all the lights spraying themselves across the sidewalks and streets and projecting their orange halo on the clouds above. But sometimes long after midnight you can feel darkness slinking around the buildings and behind the signage, slithering into the cubbyholes of doorways and stairwells. The relative quietness seems to owe more to suspense than the absence of activity, as if the city is holding its breath, waiting to see what will happen now that nobody is looking. I love the city in those hours. She seems to be saying, "Slow down, by all means. Go at your own pace—but keep your eyes open."

It was during such deep night that I would stand on the Steps chatting with the gay men who gathered there from across the city and around the world. Mention Toronto to a well-traveled gay man in San Francisco or Amsterdam in those days, and he'd respond, "Oh yeah—the Steps." That was when I'd stop by 501 to chat with Jeff and Diana behind the bar, or Chris as s/he sashayed from the closet that served as a dressing room to the little stage that backed onto the front windows.

After that, I'd head farther down Church Street. I half expected that, at some point after I'd gotten used to the out-there behavior and general weirdness of the gay bars, I might actually experience some measure of temptation to experiment. There were certainly enough "straight" men who showed up in the gay clubs looking to take a little walk on the wild side. I knew there were some who thought that's what I was doing, too, but although I didn't find the idea of queer sex repugnant, as some claimed to do, it never found a flicker of response in me.

It was what I did find night after night down around Church and Gerrard, half a dozen blocks south, that got me ruminating on the nature of my own sexuality. There were at least four or five distinct prostitution "tracks" or "strolls" within a short walk of Sanctuary. The one that occupied the block bounded by Church, Gerrard, Jarvis, and College Streets was known locally as "the high track." It was where the most expensive women plied their trade under the watchful eyes of a couple of aging outlaw bikers parked at a table in a burger joint.

The women were attractive, smart, and appeared fearless. They dressed in expensive, often gaudy "hooker gear"—that's what they called it—calculated to entice without giving anything away that could be sold. It was rare to see a young girl, in her early to mid-teens, on that highly controlled and fiercely defended stroll. No, the kiddies were elsewhere. You had to be a true pro who had paid her dues and knew her business cold to work there. Still, not many had yet hit thirty, and most were in their early to mid-twenties. There's a short shelf-life in that business.

A few claimed diagonal corners at Jarvis and Gerrard. Two groups cruised back and forth on Jarvis and College, just shy of the hotel entrances near the corner. One tall blonde and her brunette partner commanded the southeast corner of College and Church wearing complimentary outfits. They both worked for the same pimp and weren't allowed to fraternize with any of the other women.

The women I would come to know best lounged against the wall of the office of the Catholic Diocese of Toronto, on Church just above Gerrard, smoking voluptuously, their thigh-high boots with the vicious-looking spike heels crossed delicately at the ankles. My outreach partners and I referred to them gleefully as "the Church Ladies."

Robin, Tiny, Heidi, Donna, a couple of Cassandras, Franca and Gypsy, who is long out of "the trade" and my pal to this day. One slim Chinese Filipino woman whose name I don't recall, but I can still see her, pretty and self-composed as a cat. A handful of others who came and went.

It took a couple of years before I got to know their names. Until I did, they were more like icons to me than real women: mysterious, inscrutable, and yet no deeper than the polished surface. Other. This, I think, is the barbed hook in the subconscious of the consumers of pornography and prostitution—the illusion that the women involved don't exist as people with entire lives; that they appear magically without histories and cease to be the moment they are beyond the sight or reach of the men who purchase their services. This is not just sex without relationship—it's sex as the very abnegation of relationship.

They were icons, alright, and not just of some twisted vision of femaleness. What they truly represented wasn't so much "bad girls" as it was something badly broken and buried deep within me. The scenarios my imagination generated ran like slime down the danker walls of my mind.

Predictably, just getting to know their names broke the dark magic; getting to know them as people, some even as friends, dispelled it altogether. Once they became human to me, I could no longer view them merely as biddable characters in my own interior drama. It was such a relief—and they turned out to be such funny, resilient, tough women.

I had recognized the danger I was in very early on, and so had made myself a rule—and taught it to my outreach partners who came along later—that I'd never do that kind of street outreach alone. (As time went on, it became clear that doing any kind of street outreach alone, especially late at night, wasn't a great idea.) But the whole experience gave me pause.

I was as familiar with lust as anybody, so it wasn't just that. Maybe it was the visceral power of it that was different, or the very real sense of imminent peril. At any rate, I began to consider how distinct this dark attraction was from what I sought with my wife. Although there were struggles in our marriage, and we would ultimately fail, I found her desirable, too. What I desired with her was deep and growing intimacy; sex was important but only one mode of expressing both desire and the connection it sought. The sexual desire I had for her and the desire I'd had for the women on the stroll was apparently the same thing, but in fact radically different. They were like two vectors hurrying away from a single point in opposite directions. And neither mode of desire had cancelled out the other. As long as those women were nameless, what they called up in me was in fact a complete perversion and repudiation of what I believed human sexuality was supposed to be.

At the time, I believed a homosexual act was sinful in itself, and also that it was prompted by the essential sinfulness in the world that results from the fall. Like many others, I came to think of this as "brokenness"—the world itself was broken, human affairs at all levels were broken, people were broken; none of it or them worked as they were supposed to. And now, the fundamental brokenness of my own self, particularly my sexuality, was no longer theoretical. The reality of it struck me with a force that was new and deeply disconcerting.

The more I considered it, the more I could see just how broken I was. I began to see how frequently and casually I objectified women all around me, especially ones I didn't know, and not just the women on the stroll. I could identify my entirely selfish attitudes and drives even within the sanctified boundaries of marital sexuality. Through the years, as my marriage deteriorated and I felt more and more emotionally isolated, it got worse and worse, until a glimpse of an attractive woman walking down the street could prompt an attack of desire that struck me like a punch to the guts.

And I was powerless to stop it. Any of it. I could and did resist acting on it, but it didn't change.

It got me thinking differently about my queer friends. How realistic was it to say, "Sucks to be you. You'll just have to be celibate for the rest of your life if you want to follow Jesus"? Some people have the capacity for lengthy celibacy, but I wasn't at all sure that I did. Resisting temptation became harder and harder the lonelier I felt as my marriage fell apart, until there were moments when I was terrified that I'd run out and do something crazy. By God's grace I never did, but it was surely a near thing. It also became harder to trust that "Just say no" was God's one-size-fits-all answer to people he had made without the ability to wear something off the rack.

So now there was this: my sexuality was broken; the sexuality of my queer friends was broken. Were we essentially, in the eyes of God, any different?

7

Christ in Dark Places

THE HOT FUNK IN Neil's bedroom was so thick it was hard to breathe. It must have been ninety degrees in there, the windows streaming and the radiator steaming. He lay wide-eyed and staring at nothing, so tangled in his sheets that it looked like some marauder passing through had bound him. I could see at a glance what my nose had told me already: the sheets were copiously stained with broad smears of mucous-y yellow and brown. He must have thrashed his way into that state in a mad panic, but now he just lay quivering, his jaw and mind both unhinged.

I couldn't bring myself to sit on the bed, but squatted beside it, calling his name and talking him back from wherever it was he'd gone. Once he knew I was there—"Oh, it's you," he mewed, and relief washed the terror from his face—I set about setting him free. Stripped of the sheets and his filthy pajamas, he lay unaware or unashamed of his nakedness.

Neil was dying of AIDS. His partner had died too, a couple of years earlier, before Neil had even been diagnosed, but this was the mid-nineties and the epidemic was in the fullness of its slaughterhouse strength. The house was rife with pictures of the two of them: vibrant, fit, joyful men in their late thirties, running marathons, camping, raising a glass in exotic locales. It was hard to find the Neil I knew, this Neil before me, in those photos.

In the space of those short years, the athlete had been rendered a mere skeleton, the muscle and fat melted from his bones. His teeth were too big for his mouth, his eyes for his sockets; his hair lay thin and colorless, sweat-plastered across the hollows and crevasses of his skull. His skin clung fiercely to the rack of him like thin leather badly stretched and tanned. A color no one would ever call a complexion.

I ran a bath and carried him to it; a man six feet tall who was as light and brittle as a bundle of dry sticks. While he soaked, I stripped the bed and carried the mess downstairs to the laundry room, giving thanks that the paid support worker would take it from there. Back upstairs, I sponged him gently from head to foot. He was too weak to do even that. And then I carried him back to the freshly made bed, dressed him in clean pajamas, and tucked him in.

I've written and published this story before, in my first book, *God in the Alley*. I've told it often too, so it feels a little like cheating to relate it yet again. But what happened next was one of the most profound, perspective-altering moments in my life; a pivotal moment, it would turn out, in my long trudge to deeper understanding not only of the matter at hand in this book, but in many other areas of my thinking. So it seems I have to tell it one more time.

I had come to the city core with the clear belief that my mission was to be the presence of Christ in dark places. I discovered, over and over, that he'd got there before me.

The nerve!

In those early days I was prepared to preach at the drop of a hat. In fact, I'd had to specifically promise Betty Ann, the AIDS Committee of Toronto volunteer coordinator, that I would resist all temptation to do so while volunteering. I understood that many of the clients of ACT had experienced only rejection and judgment from church people, so it made sense to me. But it was still an exercise in self-control to restrain myself.

While cleaning Neil up and tucking him back in bed, it had struck me with revelatory force that *this* was what it meant to be "the presence of Christ"—I was literally washing the filth from

Neil as Jesus had washed the dust from his disciples' feet at the Last Supper. But there was still greater revelation yet to come.

Sitting now boldly on the side of Neil's bed, I asked if he wanted to pray. It was a habit we had gotten into, at his request, despite the fact that Neil was not a Christian. He blended some vestiges of the Mormonism he'd had to abandon when he came out with a variety of new age and mystical elements; what he ended up with was a malleable pastiche of spirituality that was all his own.

"Yes," he murmured, and fell silent.

I mumbled some more or less rote prayer, all the while feeling quite exalted by the thought that here I was, being the presence of Christ!

When I was done, Neil's breathing was low and steady, his eyes closed and his limbs still. I sat for a while to be sure he was asleep and was just about to stand up to leave when, without opening his eyes or moving at all, he began to pray.

He addressed himself to no one by name. He asked nothing for himself, this dying man, but instead pronounced word upon whispered word, halting sentence upon sentence of blessing over me. He gave thanks for my friendship, lauded my character and affirmed my actions in his own life and in the broader world.

Before very long he lapsed into silence. I sat stunned, unmoving. The silence lengthened until I was once again sure he had drifted into sleep. And once again, as I was about to stand, he spoke.

"In the name of Jesus," he said faintly but clearly. And the words seemed to float like a bright banner in that heavy air.

I had been reading the words of Jesus in Matthew's Gospel not long before, and they came back to me now:

> I was hungry and you gave me food,
> I was thirsty and you gave me drink,
> I was a stranger and you welcomed me,
> I was naked and you clothed me,
> I was sick and you visited me,
> I was in prison and you came to me . . .

Truly, I say to you,
as you did it to one of the least of these my brothers,
you did it to me.
(Matt 25:35, 36, 40.)

It may seem so obvious as to be unremarkable to some now, but I can hardly overstate the impact the realization had on me: *Neil had been the presence of Christ to me.* And it wasn't just Neil. I was surrounded by people who were hungry, thirsty, strangers, humiliated, sick, or in prison. Jesus was everywhere! Some days, I'd literally trip over him sleeping on the front steps as I left Sanctuary.

An alcoholic Blackfoot man named Marcel; a street-involved woman named Angel; Lila; Bear; Gypsy; Cliff; Iggy; these and dozens upon dozens more through the years were, in specific moments as clear if less dramatic than that with Neil, the presence of Christ to me. He still shows up so regularly that it has become somewhat routine, if that can be imagined, and I have to rouse my soul to recognize and rejoice in his presence. Surely you can see how powerfully this change of perspective impacted my relationships. It defused some of my ego, taught me that sometimes receiving is more blessed than giving, showed me how "serving" can be a way of clinging to power, relieved me of the pressure to try to convert people, allowed me real friendships instead of quasi-hierarchical weirdness, and much, much more.

I was preaching in churches on Sunday mornings a lot in those days—Sanctuary's gathering has always been in the early evening—and as mentioned, I trotted out my Neil story frequently. Neil had died within days of that encounter. I had not only lost a friend who had become genuinely dear to me, but his prayer of blessing were the last words I'd heard him speak. I could rarely tell it without fighting back tears; Kleenex and sniffles generally abounded in the congregations. People were genuinely touched. Some said my account changed their perspective, too. Even in very conservative congregations, the fact that Neil had been gay didn't seem to matter, although I did have to articulate the whole *Neil was the presence of Christ* idea carefully.

Then came what, for years afterward, I considered the greatest preaching debacle of my life.

I didn't know any other evangelical Christians who were doing outreach in gay communities at that time, apart, perhaps, from those disastrous and ill-named "gay recovery" ministries, if they could be termed "outreach." But spiritually hungry queer folk were, here and there, beginning to show up in churches, sidling into back row seats and keeping their heads down until they could tell whether or not the gamble of disclosure would be worth it. Some of those churches genuinely wanted to be welcoming, but usually had no idea how.

I was invited to speak one Sunday morning at such a church in another city. They wanted me to offer a biblical perspective on homosexuality; I thought, "Oh boy, here we go." I was under no illusions that I had figured anything out, but at least I had been thinking about it. So along I went.

I told my Neil story. So far, so good—eyes being dabbed, noses discreetly blown. Then we dug into Romans chapter 1, which many would consider to be the most definitive of the "prohibitive passages." I don't recall exactly what I had to say about Paul's diatribe on the moral state of his world, and God's releasing of men and women to the consequences of their own behavior. As I don't usually make let alone keep sermon notes, I have no way of checking. Given the response, I'm pretty sure that any recording that may have been made has long since been wiped clean.

I might have said something about the fact that the sexual stuff was only one aspect of a whole slew of behaviors that clearly really bug God. Might have pointed out that some of Paul's language seems to indicate consciously extreme sexual adventurism rather than committed relationship, that he was probably referring to specific commonly known activities in contemporary culture. I would certainly not, at that point in my journey, have said anything to justify same-gender sex. I'm pretty sure I would have observed that I had no trouble at all finding several of my own behaviors among the offenses listed. (Again, I urge you to check out *Romans Disarmed*, by Keesmaat and Walsh, for a far more cogent and deeply grounded exegesis of this passage. Among other things, they develop its imperial context in a way that completely escaped me.)

And I know that I definitely complained about the artificial and disruptive chapter division inserted many centuries later. Because Paul's entire chapter 1 argument comes in for a landing on chapter 2, verse 1:

> Therefore you have no excuse, O man, every one of you who judges. For in passing judgment on another you condemn yourself, because you, the judge, practice the very same things.

In judging queer people, out of that whole list of behaviors, we straight Christians were doing exactly what Paul warns against: judging others when we ourselves were guilty. Throughout the rest of chapter 2 and through most of chapter 3 he continues to build his case, layer by discouraging layer, until concluding, "*There is no distinction*, for *all* have sinned and fall short of the glory of God" (italics mine).

Thank God he didn't stop there, but in the next phrase went straight to the antidote: ". . . and are justified by his grace as a gift, through the redemption that is in Christ Jesus" (Rom 3:23, 24).

I think I left it there, an admittedly unsatisfying conclusion as to whether or not it was okay to be queer, but pretty sweet when you considered that *all* applied equally to *have sinned* and *are justified*.

Nobody complained to me right after the service, in fact there was some really positive response, but by the time I completed the hour-and-a-half drive home an elder of the church was calling wanting explanations. A few people had apparently got all in a twist about what they thought I was sneakily implying and made enough noise that the elders had to respond. For the first time, somebody was objecting that I had compared a gay man dying of AIDS to Christ.

I was embarrassed, defensive, and apologetic. Causing an upset in another church had never been on my agenda. I'd only addressed the subject because I was asked to, and then had done so as honestly as I was able, admitting both my interpretive struggles and personal foibles. So, yes, I back-pedaled. And, as mentioned, for years afterward I shook my head whenever I thought about what a disastrous job I had done that day.

I continued to tell the story about Neil, though, almost always to a very positive response. I was so mortified by the upset I had caused that I was careful not to pose publicly the questions that continued to bombard me. I wondered, every now and then, how that particular sermon had gone so spectacularly sideways.

There was never any specific moment of clarity, but over time—a long time—the realization trickled through:

As far as my kind of church was concerned, a dying Neil might be acceptable, even touching, as "the presence of Christ," but a living, gay Neil was not acceptable as a follower of Christ. Talk about theological dissonance!

8

Must Not All Love Derive from Him?

"WE'RE GETTING MARRIED!" BETTY Ann announced gleefully, her incredible blue eyes sparkling with delight. She had invited me for coffee to tell me something important and had wasted no time in getting to it.

"Oh, BA, that's awesome! Congratulations!"

I gave her a big hug and meant all of it. I'd heard her talk about Nicki for a couple of years, going back to volunteer orientation, when they'd just started dating. In the interim, we'd become fast friends. Betty Ann had a razor mind and wit, gentled by an enormously compassionate heart. She'd related her struggles acknowledging then embracing her sexual orientation as a very young woman growing up devoutly Catholic. I'd told her not only about my fundamentalist background, but my continuing attempts to let God out of the successive boxes I'd placed him in. She had steered me through Roxanne's death and the early days of my relationship with Neil. She'd helped me understand which of my attitudes and words would be offensive to queer people, and why. And in my volunteer work with ACT, she had always affirmed me being absolutely transparent about who I was and why I was there.

The reality that my own sexuality was as broken as anyone's, and that both Jesus and Paul had actually meant it when they said, "Don't judge anyone or you'll be judged yourself," had sunk into my thinking deeply enough that they were no longer just theoretical precepts. While I still couldn't genuinely affirm same-gender sexual relationships, nor did I have any idea what to do with trans people, I at least knew that I didn't really need to do either. It wasn't like the world was waiting in breathless suspense until I got it all figured out. It wasn't up to me to set the rules for queer living. What was up to me was this: love.

What I was discovering was that, when you love people instead of trying to figure out how to fit them into your theological/philosophical/societal or even economic frameworks, you begin to empathize with them instead of worrying about whether they're right or innocent or deserving. Love dismantles the lover's instinctive arrogance.

Betty Ann was such a good person that loving her was easy. (Much more so than some of my friends in the Sanctuary community!) What loving her meant was simply that I wanted to see her showered with the very best gifts that life and God—or as she would say, "the Universe"—had to offer. I wanted to do whatever I could to facilitate that kind of blessing. Focusing on Jesus's crystal-clear command to "love one another!" instead of worrying about whether or not I was right had got me thinking in some other directions, too.

For instance, since God is love, must not all love derive from him? (Or "her," BA would say.) If he was the source of all love, he must surely affirm all love, else he would be denying himself. Wouldn't he? A child's love for a puppy—he'd affirm that, right? Likewise, obviously, the various iterations of familial love, friend love, and so on. I was pretty sure he affirmed my love for my wife, as fractured as it was. He affirmed it in the midst of my many non-loving or even anti-loving sinful attitudes and actions. Sometimes it was hard even for me to know what, precisely, in my relationships came from love, and what came from selfishness, ego, or insecurity. Fortunately, God knew, and he kept affirming the love even when it was blended in with a slurry of the other stuff.

So, I thought, for BA and my other queer friends, God would certainly affirm and bless the love one had for another. It seemed to me that he would affirm so much else that came from that love—tenderness, self-sacrifice, generosity, commitment . . . At what point did the affirmation stop, I wondered? Was holding hands okay? Hugging? A kiss? Was it only physical expressions? At what point would God, if he was inclined to speak up, say, "Okay kids, better stop it right there"?

It was a foolishly legalistic way to think about it, I knew, but I couldn't help myself. I wondered. I thought, knowing my own heart as I did, that if he'd been inclined to speak to me in similar circumstance, he'd often say, "Whoa, hold up there. This is just all about you now, sonny boy, and that's not right."

One thing was clear: God kept loving and blessing me, regardless. Would he do less for anyone else?

So it was easy for me to be genuinely thrilled for Betty Ann and Nicki, and to hope and trust that God would bless them with every good gift. But it turned out that the marriage announcement itself was only part of BA's excitement.

She leaned across her coffee, both hands wrapping the mug, those eyes fairly dancing. A smile she struggled to contain.

"And we want you to marry us."

My heart sank. I'd known somebody would ask eventually and dreaded the moment. The fact that it turned out to be Betty Ann made it even worse.

"Oh . . . BA, I'm so honored. Really, really honored and touched that you would ask *me*." A straight, pretty conservative Christian guy, is what I meant. And I really meant the rest of what I said, too. It was incredibly (and typically) generous of her. I'm sure I gulped and grimaced a bit before continuing.

"But I can't. I wish . . . but I can't!"

BA's smile was frozen in place now, and the sparkle in her eyes dimmed. They went flat as I tried lamely to explain. I could see disappointment then a puzzled hurt settle on her features, despite her best efforts to appear unconcerned and unaffected.

Although I truly didn't believe her relationship with Nicki was any more or less sinful in essence than mine with my wife,

Christian marriage was the final, unpassable border as far as my theological understanding and convictions were concerned.

I had by this point had many a conversation with gay and lesbian people who wanted to know what I thought God thought about their relationships with their partners. It was pretty clear to me that promiscuity, regardless of the genders involved, was contrary to the plan. Sex is holy, a covenant made with our bodies, and meant to be an expression of deep and deepening relationship, protected by and respected with unbroken fidelity—an expression, in other words, of the unshakable, undeviating love of the Creator for the people he created, and of the intimacy into which he constantly invites them.

But since all love flows from him, I thought any two people who loved each other should value, nurture, and rejoice in that love, giving thanks to the one who was its source. I'd tell them that whatever was truly love in them, God would bless. That, obviously, he was willing to heal but could not bless what was broken, a willful disobedience, contrary to his good and perfect will for us—and that all this applied as much to straight as to queer couples.

If pressed, I'd admit that I thought same-gender sex was inherently broken, a divergence from created order. Some, including BA, were uncomfortable with the idea that queerness was an expression of brokenness, even when I stressed my conviction that my own sexuality was all busted up and divergent too, at least in its particulars.

The clever ones, like her, would say things like, "Yeah, but you're saying some aspects of your relationship and actions are sinful, whereas with me, it's who I am that's sinful." I didn't know how to answer that effectively. It wasn't what I *felt* like I meant, but it sure sounded, even to me, like that's what I was saying.

At the end of the day, I'd say to my friends, try as we might to do the right thing, we all need to trust in his limitless grace. As I'd find years later, as my first marriage sputtered to its painful conclusion, nobody ever found peace by justifying themselves, their actions or choices. Peace can only be found by resting in God's grace.

I can't tell you what to do, I would tell my friends. You need to listen to him for yourself. Live with all the integrity you can. Put God first. All I can tell you is that God will treat you with more love and grace than any human being ever has.

Having found that exhaustive parsing of those prohibitive passages gave me no peace or place to rest, no clear direction, I'd set them aside. It was only the story of creation, in the first few chapters of Genesis, that gave me a little plot to stand on.

The account of the creation of humanity made it clear that God had made male and female, both, as an expression of his own image. Joining them together—marriage—completed the image of God reflected in humanity. Their distinct but complementary nature was a picture of the character of the Trinity, completed by their fruitfulness together in the creation of children. It's partly why, despite having referred to God as "he" and "him" so far in this book, I've come to believe that the Holy Spirit in particular is expressed by human femaleness. God the Father, Holy Spirit the Mother, Jesus the Son. (There's lots of other biblical support for that, by the way.) The intended lifelong nature of "cleaving" to each other, and "becoming one flesh" illustrated the insoluble and intimate nature of the Trinity and would also become figures of God's loving faithfulness to his people, and his desire for intimacy with them.

Marriage, then, needed to be between a woman and a man, in order to fulfill the image. It was what God meant by marriage—the joining of male to female. I'd come to think that covenanted same-gender relationships might well be within the scope of grace, but it wasn't marriage as God intended us to understand it. It was some kind of second-tier thing.

I watched BA's face fall as I stumbled through my long-winded and complicated explanation. She was so gracious. Far more so than I would have been. I wouldn't have blamed her in that moment, nor would I have been surprised, if she'd simply stood up and walked out. Trying to recover at least some small kindness in it, I babbled on.

"I can't marry you, but I'd be honored to come to the wedding. And I want to bless you in any way that I can."

Because that's what God does, I meant. Blesses us in the midst of our brokenness. I did want to bless her and Nicki, and I did believe God would bless them, too. I meant it kindly, but it felt so condescending to say it. It sounded so unsatisfactory to my own ears—all of it—that I could hardly imagine what it must sound like to her.

BA was the truly grace-filled one in that conversation.

"Well," she said slowly, with a sad little smile, "would you pray a blessing for us at the reception?"

Felt like she'd thrown me a lifeline just as I was about to go down for the third time. Of course, I said. Yes. Yes.

9

Love Has Kept Me Searching

Theological dissonance.

A lack of harmony between what your beliefs tell you you're supposed to do, and what your soul tells you is the character of God. That awful feeling you get when you're doing what you believe to be right, but it feels wrong. When "loving" people actually seems to damage them.

An abiding theological dissonance is a sign that there's something wrong. Might be my attitude or my theology. My unwillingness to admit I might be wrong; my unwillingness to submit to God; my laziness or faithlessness in seeking better, deeper answers.

Sometimes a theological dissonance causes us to waffle and finally ditch our convictions; our personal integrity takes a hit, and so may our trust in God. Sometimes it causes us to turn hard and even angry, doubling down on those convictions until the quiet voice of what might be grace, or love, or mercy is throttled by habitual harshness. We lean harder on *the rules* and lose our freedom and our tenderness. Neither course leads to peace, a restful, fruitful integration of mind and spirit, nor to the expression of true grace or graceful truth.

I had a bad case of it.

I couldn't escape the niggling thought that my perspective relegated BA—not just "queer people," but my dear friend

BA!—to second-class status in the eyes of God. Collateral damage in the war between heaven and hell. Although I couldn't get past the Genesis version of marriage, the result seemed a little off somehow. No, not just "off"—terrifically unsatisfying. For all the biblical sense I thought it made, it just didn't seem like God to say, "Sorry. Luck of the draw. You happen to be part of that small minority that can't fit into my system, so I got nothin' for you. I'll keep forgiving you, but . . ."

God doesn't turn away anyone who seeks. He raises people up as they trust in him; he doesn't abandon them to their fate. He's a Redeemer. He takes a broken thing and doesn't just fix it—he transforms it into a new thing of strength and beauty. I believed that. Just couldn't see how he was doing it with queer folk.

That's where I was stuck for more than a decade. God loves you and extends his grace to you, I kept telling my queer friends, just like he does me. We're no better and no worse than each other. But, the garden, see, the "created order" thing. . . . I'm afraid marriage isn't for you. No, I have no idea how you're supposed to live it, then. Do your best. . . .

The more I said it, the more tired I got of saying it. Repeating it didn't strengthen my conviction; it sounded lamer each time.

Dissonance.

I'm telling my story now because, through the years, I've had a lot of tender-hearted, well-meaning Christian people with conservative convictions in this matter come visit me. It seems more come every year. They're struggling, too. When queer folk show up in their lives or congregations, they want to truly love and embrace them. They wish they could freely affirm and bless same-gender relationships, unions, and marriages. They want to fully welcome transgender people. But their convictions about what they believe the Bible says won't allow it. They would never say it out loud, maybe can't even admit it to themselves, but they're wondering how they—small, weak, finite people—could be feeling a greater urge to love and embrace and lift up queer people than God apparently does.

Theological dissonance.

The only constructive stance in the midst of such doubt and internal disharmony is one of faith. Being willing to say, "I don't know. I think I know some things, but not that. I'll just have to keep wondering, thinking, listening. Staying open. I trust God will sort it out or redeem it in the end." We learn to hold our convictions lightly, knowing that we are ridiculously fallible, trusting that God will reveal what we need to know in his time, and that meanwhile, if we love first and always, he will keep us from doing too much harm.

What keeps us seeking, or what wakes us up in the first place, I've noticed, is not usually intellectual curiosity, a desire for clearer doctrine, or a hunger for abstract truth. It's people. Real flesh-and-blood people who are right next to us, walking around in our lives, claiming space in our hearts and so also in our thoughts. People of iron-clad conservative conviction begin to rethink their position, not because of news items or social media campaigns or theological arguments, but because a daughter comes out; because a son says, "Mom and Dad, I'm really your daughter." It's not a desire to be right that opens us up, starts and keeps us seeking. It's love.

Some people will dismiss this perspective out of hand. They'll claim that when people change their convictions because of their love for a child, a sibling, a friend, they're making truth itself subjective—making truth to be whatever they want it to be, instead of what it actually is. Truth, they will say, is more important than love.

Such were the families of the men I met years ago on the Steps. It was the rule rather than the exception then that families of queer men and women cut them off once they publicly identified themselves—even families with no particular faith perspective or conviction. Because everybody knew that it was just wrong. It just was.

And those men lived in the knowledge that they were condemned. Condemned by their families, condemned by society at large, condemned by God. Condemned despite their urgent longing and best efforts to be other than they were. I am haunted still by the agony I heard in those voices, whispering out of the shadows behind the brick pillars in the middle of the night, the resigned helplessness, the conviction of impending and eternal doom.

How harsh, how rigid must such a God be? Can this be the same God who so loved the world that he gave his only Son? Why would he not, if it was needed, heal or release or in some fashion change ones whose confession was so abject?

Listen: *without love, God's truth cannot be known.*

"God is love," John says. Not "God is truth." Jesus's new commandment was not "Know the truth!" or "Be right!" It was "Love one another."

I'm glad he didn't just say "be loving." He made it clear that love is an action from one person to another. It's not an abstract concept but a thoroughly pragmatic instruction. It has to be applied in the real world, in real time, between real people. It's the only means by which we can live rightly. It's the only mechanism by which we can attain a practical unity—agreement will always fail, for we will always find some point of disagreement. If we are not compelled by love, the "truth" we find will be no truth at all.

By all means let us keep seeking truth, but let's not fool ourselves that we can ever be certain that we have found it perfectly and objectively. We're far too human for that.

I'm so grateful for those families who, when one of their own declares themselves, leap lovingly into the void. They keep loving and embracing: they suspend judgment even when doing so leaves them morally disoriented and subject to this new dissonance. I'm not speaking here of the growing numbers, Christian and otherwise, for whom sexual orientation or gender identity are simply no issue. I mean people who have previously tended to think, "Well, it's just wrong." Some who have based that thinking on strongly held opinions about what the Bible says. Instinctively they have recognized that love is revealing the weakness of their understanding of truth. It's not that they've concluded the Bible is mistaken; like me, they suspect their interpretation of it must be flawed.

It's love that keeps me still seeking, desiring a better, deeper, more loving understanding of that which is true. It's because I loved BA, and Neil, and other queer friends, that I longed for a "better truth," one that was more consistent with the infinitely loving, gracious and, yes, true God. I think I've found it, but it's been a long, long journey.

Queer people are way over-represented statistically in homeless and street-involved populations, a reflection of the degree to which they did and still do experience trauma and rejection by family and society. Combine that fact with the knowledge that Sanctuary, my community and workplace since 1992, is just a stone's throw from the traditional heart of Toronto's gay neighborhood and it will come as no surprise that I've been close to hundreds of LGTBQ2+ people through the years. Dozens of queer people I've known have been murdered or died far too young as a result of AIDS or addictions. The memories of them have also kept me searching.

As I was working on this book, Toronto police announced their arrest of a man who was ultimately charged with and pled guilty to the murders and dismemberment of eight gay men. People in the gay community have been reporting the mysterious disappearances of gay men for years, with, they feel, little interest shown by the cops until just recently. Even in our "enlightened" age, it's hard to believe anyone would willingly choose such a fraught and dangerous orientation.

Perhaps for someone untouched by such tragedies it would be easy to say something like, "If you play with fire you'll get burned." But these precious people weren't playing with fire. They were just backed into inescapable corners because of who they are. And if this is the kind of thing that has happened to people you love, and keeps on happening, it's pretty clear that something needs to change.

While preparing to write this chapter, I wrote this in an email to a couple of dear friends:

> Whether you're aware of it or not, loving and being loved
> by the two of you through all these years has been key in
> this regard. In fact, I would say there are no others I have

thought of so often as I've struggled, at any given time, with these issues. In a phrase, wanting better answers for two people I love has kept me searching.

These two are not the only ones. There are many who have nudged me onward, whose faith and faithfulness have inspired me, even as they have challenged my perceptions and thinking. Their stories and voices have been prophetic to me, dismantling my constructs about the Bible, people, and God himself, and revealing a more spacious truth and a greater Creator than I had previously known. Revealing, too, I have come to believe, a clearer view of the future God has planned for us.

One such prophet in my life has been a woman named Janice. In her sixties now, she is a short, comfortable, grandmotherly figure with glasses, shoulder-length greying hair, and a voice pitched low in both tone and volume. She serves on Sanctuary's board of directors, and preaches periodically on Sundays in a gentle, scholarly manner. She's also something of an evangelist, routinely bringing new people to the Sanctuary community, where she's confident they will be received and loved in the name of Jesus.

Janice began life as John.

Even as a little boy, John was a disappointment to his father, a successful businessman, and church organist and choir director in his spare time. John was very small, physically not strong, and not at all interested in the usual boyhood games and sports. When John began to have epileptic seizures—a debilitating lifelong challenge—his father would yell at him as if they were the little boy's fault.

Janice remembers little John, at five years of age, already feeling ripped off because he hadn't been born a girl—he felt that the body he'd been given was second best. This gender dysphoria (the deep and distressing sense one's body is the wrong gender) would continue and only increase over the next thirty-five years.

Still, John completed high school and went off to university. He began to read the Bible because he thought it might help him with his studies of ancient history. His father's "faith," despite the church activities, had been nominal at best; the power of God's Word surprised and shook John. When I asked Janice why the

Psalms in particular had so affected young John, she said simply, "They were sublime." This confused young man became a Christian, and for the first time had something real to anchor him.

He married a childhood friend. Having completed his undergrad, he was motivated by his new faith to begin studies toward a master of divinity degree. Over the next several years, he and Sara had three children. Their eldest daughter was severely handicapped and unable to communicate verbally, requiring feeding through a tube in her stomach. Between a demanding course load, part-time work, and a fraught family life, the stresses grew. He kept hoping the dysphoria would go away; if anything, it got worse. He had cross-dressed in secret off and on since he was a child and began to do so again. Sara didn't know, although it was obvious that her husband was deeply and continually depressed.

John's faith was real. He knew in his heart, and would never doubt through all that followed, that God loved him. But not a whisper of an answer did he get to his impossible situation.

John and Sara's marriage lasted fifteen years. Janice says Sara was a wonderful person, going beyond what anyone—especially in the early nineties—could have expected. When John finally confessed to her what was going on, she even for a time allowed him to cross-dress at home. Ultimately, though, the increasing pressure meant that the situation was untenable for both of them. Sara told their families and the family doctor about her husband's struggle. The family wrote him off; the doctor suggested he go to the Clarke Institute for assessment and perhaps acceptance into the gender-reassignment program.

Sara asked John to move out. He did, and took the first concrete steps toward becoming Janice.

Janice enrolled in the program at the Clarke and, after a short stay in a Salvation Army hostel, moved into a room in a crack house. She stayed in that rat-infested hole, where a herd of addicts came and went and all shared one filthy washroom, sleeping on a lawn chair, for eighteen months. She had lived in typical middle-class accommodations until then; the profound poverty of her circumstances now was yet another shock to her system.

Through all this, Janice's parents and sister maintained their distant silence. Children's Aid Society, which had gotten involved with her children, prohibited her from seeing them. (CAS no longer sees a transgender parent as dangerous to the kids.) Not long after, Sara remarried and moved, with the children, from the Toronto area to the United States. Street preachers would glance in Janice's direction as she passed by and proclaim that she was going to hell. Others told her she was crazy. An uncle and brother-in-law visited her once at her room; disturbed by the penury and danger they saw, they offered enough financial support for her to move to a safer, cleaner place. Apart from that, and a few new acquaintances from the groups at the Clarke, Janice was journeying through this new, harrowing reality alone.

And yet not alone.

She says now, "I don't know how I'd have been without my faith. I made a real effort to cleave to God. It was like riding a roller coaster, holding tight to him."

After three years of counselling and hormone therapy at the Clarke, three years of living publicly as a woman in a man's body, she was approved for surgery. She woke up from it totally thrilled with her "new" physical self. For the first time in her life, she thought, "At last my soul is in line with my body!" The dysphoria was gone forever.

As you can imagine, it still hasn't been an easy path. Some years after the surgery, she received an unexpected call from her parents. Her father was ill. They wanted Janice to know that she shouldn't visit and wouldn't be invited to either of their funerals. Even in the gay community, transgender people are sometimes treated prejudicially; it's worse still in the world at large. Being a transgender woman and epileptic, at times severely so, has made it hard for her to get and keep work.

As a child, she knew that the truth of her would come out some day, and she would be rejected. That prophecy has come to pass, and still holds to a significant degree, but she's also become a truly important and beloved person in our community—she says coming to Sanctuary is the most important thing that's happened in her life since transitioning. She's finally found the family she never really had.

We sat together in a busy café as she filled in the details of her story, which I had previously known only in generalities. As our interview came to a close, she ruminated a bit, looking back over her complicated, painful path.

"If I hadn't been transgender, I would have become like my family," she said. Faithless, she meant. Dismissive of the poor and rejecters of the people Christ came to save. And she smiled her gentle smile, grateful to know who she is as a woman and as a follower of Jesus.

With people like Janice in my life, it's no wonder that I've kept on searching.

10

A Little Sliver of an Opening

I COULD COUNT ON the fingers of one hand the number of times I feel like God has spoken to me, in the sense of articulating a clear message that I heard (sort of) as a voice saying words. I don't seek it, as I believe there's a significant danger that you'll hear what you want to hear; and anyway, he's already spoken at length in the Bible, and he speaks all the time in the world around me and through the voices of people in my life. On those rare occasions when I think he has spoken up in the more direct sense, he's always been laconic to an almost infuriating degree, planting a thought or a question then clamming up again while I spend weeks, months, or even years trying to figure out, "What, exactly, am I supposed to do with that?"

His little "Well, I use *you*, don't I?" jab after my lunch with John was one of those. More frequently, but still rarely, an expression from Scripture seems to drop unbidden into my mind as if launched from above. I know it won't be convincing—it can't be, really—to anyone else, but on those occasions I feel quite persuaded that God is specifically drawing my attention to something, and that the thoughts that immediately accompany the experience are a sort of gift that comes from outside of myself. Which doesn't mean, of course, that my subsequent interpretation or application of that word is faultless; just that I have the feeling that God has planted a seed that will grow, if I pay attention to it.

In 2012, while I was still the executive director of Sanctuary, and having completed twenty years of life and work in that demanding yet profoundly fulfilling environment, the board granted me a sabbatical. I spent a week of it on the Isle of Wight off the south coast of England. Staying in the small harbor town of Ryde, I walked back and forth about ten miles each day to Quarr Abbey, originally a Cistercian monastery established in 1132 before being rebooted by French Benedictines in 1901.

I had a few purposes in mind. Spiritual retreat was at the top of the list, and in an environment that was unfamiliar enough that I wouldn't be able to rely on any of my usual reference points. As one whose heritage was Protestant and evangelical and having spent most of my adult life involved in North American, urban, street-level ministry, I thought that a Catholic monastery where the liturgy of hours was observed in bucolic English countryside sloping down to the sea would do the trick. I also wanted to observe the character of that community's life together, as I believe the gospel can only be lived out fully in community. And I wanted to get my feet and legs in shape for the week to follow, when I'd be hiking the coast of Cornwall with my brother Dave, who lived a short ferry ride away in Poole.

On the morning I began my daily walks back and forth between Ryde and Quarr, the phrase "Lord, open my eyes" seemed to leap out of the day's lectionary readings—another new discipline for me, and one I still practice. It wasn't so much that it seemed like a portentous *Word from the Lord* as it just sounded like a good thing to pray throughout that week. I did pray it, and God did at long last "open my eyes" in a small way, as I've recounted elsewhere (*Simply Open*, Thomas Nelson, 2014).

I had not been praying, "Lord, open my ears" or "open my mind," but there was a moment where it felt like he did that, too. A little sliver of an opening that gradually widened.

There was a multiplicity of routes between Ryde and Quarr, most of them taking me along small-town back streets, lined with hedgerows and ancient houses; on country roads bordered by grassy fields dotted with sheep and embraced by crumbling stone walls; and even, when the tide was out, over the glistening strand, strewn with kelp and dive-bombing sea birds. I varied my route as much as possible, and so on a couple occasions unintentionally found myself plodding the narrow shoulders of roads busy with automotive traffic.

It was while a steady stream of cars and trucks zoomed by a yard or so away—conditions I resented, as they seemed hardly conducive to contemplation—that, apparently out of nowhere, a verse of Scripture popped into my mind. Now, I should mention that I had not read Paul's Letter to the Galatians in I don't know how long, and that, having been mentally stuck for more than ten years in the one uneasy place described in the last chapter, I had been giving no conscious thought at all to matters of "queer theology" during my sabbatical. Thinking about it had played no part in my sabbatical plans and goals; I'd experienced no movement on these issues for so long that I had made an uncomfortable peace with the idea that this, as unsatisfactory as it was, was where I stood. *I was not thinking about this stuff at all and hadn't been for some time.*

Here's what drifted, light as a feather, into my grumbling mind: "There is neither Jew nor Greek, there is neither slave nor free, there is no male and female, for you are all one in Christ Jesus" (Gal 3:28).

"Huh," I thought. "*There is no male or female.* If God's redemptive agenda includes the eradication of gender difference, maybe gender shouldn't matter now either."

I stood still while the cars whizzed past and the thought sunk a little deeper. Hm.

If that was the way things were intended to be at the "consummation of all things," you'd expect it to be intimated somehow . . . and there it was! In the last of his visions, John sees "the holy city, new Jerusalem, coming down out of heaven from God, prepared as a bride adorned for her husband" (Rev 21:2).

I'd grown up hearing preachers expound upon the biblical concept of the church as the bride of Christ, had held forth on it myself many times, and somehow, until that moment, it had never occurred to me: in that image, used by both Paul and John, humanity is one gender—straight, biological males like me are characterized as a female, a bride!

Wild. Did it mean something or nothing? I pondered it a moment or two more, perhaps a little stupefied by the exhaust fumes and the noise, then parked the thought and started walking again.

Because, after all, I was praying "open my eyes," not "open my mind."

I had put the idea aside for the time being because, I suppose, I wanted my sabbatical to be a time of spiritual rest and nourishment for me, not a period of wrestling through theological tangles of any kind, let alone ones that mostly affected other people. Shallow, I know. Nevertheless, the little seed planted began to send out thread-like roots, seeking sustenance. It found some, a little sip here and there, and began to grow.

It was obvious that two short bits, one from Paul and one from John, were far from enough on their own, especially since I hadn't given much thought to their immediate context, not to mention their more important place within the metanarrative of Scripture as a whole. Still, it was intriguing that two dissimilar New Testament writers, expressing themselves in very different form, had something to say that appeared to harmonize so well. As you'd expect if God had something to say through them. The little seed became a seedling.

I thought about the matter hardly at all during the balance of my retreat week on the Isle of Wight, and still less during the following fabulous days of hiking the winding coastal paths and snug harbors of Cornwall. As is so often the case in England, it was wonderful in spite of the weather, not because of it.

It rained much of the time. For most of the rest, fog puddled like a thick soup on the fields just inland from the cliffs, spilling into the rifts and gorges that split the land every few miles, running down steep rocky walls thicketed with steaming greenery and widening into triangular beaches where they met the sea.

"There's a gorgeous view right over there," my brother Dave would say periodically, pointing toward a massy grey curtain of fog and drizzle. I'd peer for a minute, trying to discern something within or behind it.

"Yuh," I would say. "Spectacular."

And yet it was. Every so often, a stone Celtic cross would loom out of the mist as if leaning through time itself, its intricate patterns blurred by time and the elements; the white cylinder of a lighthouse would ghost in and out of view. The pale foamy crash of surf on the rocks below. When the rain beat back the fog a little, a ray of sun forcing its way through the clouds far out to sea might burnish a bright spot on the pitted pewter plate. Massive boulders hoary with lichen stood on the cliff rims gazing toward the new world. Wooden fishing boats thick with generations of paint lay pulled up on the hard, beyond reach of the tide in the little hamlets near water's edge. Nets and bright buoys hanging on the sides of stone cottages.

In the towns, ancient churches and pubs, rich inside with dark glowing wood. Stone, everywhere stone: pocked, cracked, mossy—wood rots at a fantastic rate in an atmosphere so constantly sodden. More boats leaning wearily against the quay when at ebb tide or bobbing on the moorings farther out in the harbor.

You'd think, in such weather, that the footpaths would be sparsely populated, but the Brits are a perverse and lunatic bunch. We encountered dozens every day, plowing their cheerful way up and down the coastal footpaths, bulbous-backed with packs beneath their plastic ponchos.

Each evening, after a long day of walking followed by supper in pubs which may well represent the very apex of human achievement, we'd take a bus back to the camping area where we'd left our tents and car. These camping areas, without exception, were in small soggy fields of bright grass rented out for the purpose by a farmer.

One evening we sat on the open upper deck of a bus, a dozen of us, while it wound its way along the narrow roads. All that could be seen was the narrow ribbon of asphalt for a short distance ahead and behind, the hedgerows bordering the road, and a featureless sea of silvery fog blanketing everything else. When it started to drizzle again, I stood up and addressed my fellow travelers.

"Why are we sitting up here?" I asked. "There are three times as many of us up here, in the open, in the rain, in the cold, than there are sitting warm and dry below. There's nothing to see here, people! It's all just fog! What's wrong with us?"

I'd never before met half the people I was speaking to. They looked at me, surprised, gazed around at the dim featureless scene I was gesturing toward, and began to chuckle at themselves. But nobody went below. Not one.

"Well," Dave explained later on, "you've paid your fee and want to get your money's worth, don't you? Want to see the sights when you're on hols. No point sitting all snug if you can't see but rain on the window."

"Why does he keep rattling on about this?" you may be asking, and I wouldn't blame you. This isn't supposed to be a travelogue. And yet it is a travelogue of sorts, the tale of a journey.

Here's why: the sun did come out. Taking just a little peek now and then, at first, then pushing the clouds aside for longer looks, until at last, as we were investigating the abandoned mine heads of nineteenth-century Cornish tin works, it sent them scudding across the sky and out to sea.

When the sun appeared, even if only for a few moments, it granted some clarity to the scene. It burned off a little of the fog; then a little more; and then it fled entirely.

That's how this aspect of the biblical narrative began to clarify for me, after a long period of navigating a very foggy route: a moment here, a moment there, then the mist between those moments dissolved, too. There will always be clouds, but eventually they went from low, grey, and opaque to high and white, dotting a great blue expanse.

11

Somebody Has to Be Wrong

A SUBSTANTIVE CHANGE IN one's understanding of almost anything usually requires a paradigm shift. Whether it's a fresh fact, an experience, or a relationship, something causes us to look at the problem that has stymied us from a different perspective than we have viewed it previously.

I had long since become suspicious of theological systems. (I use the word "systems" in its commonly understood sense, not as a technical theological term.) It was fascinating as well as sad to me that the body of Christ in this world was segmented and divided into camps that vociferously defended their doctrines against each other, when Jesus's prayer was "that they may become perfectly one, so that the world may know that you sent me" (John 17:23). There was—and is—no end to argument, and each party or denomination seemed so certain of its essential rightness. Defining ourselves by the differences in our systems was defeating our Master's purpose for us instead of leading us toward it.

Look, where there are divergent views, somebody has to be wrong. I'd grown up in a doctrinal system that had radically shaped my view of both the Bible and the world around me. As a very young guy, I had been able to articulate and defend that body of doctrine—and if I may brag a little, I'd been able to do so with unusual ability for someone my age. It all made perfect sense to me.

Until my "unassailable" defences began to crack. Reality intruded, questions arose. My view shifted, and suddenly many of my certainties began to wobble. It doesn't really matter now what the specific issues were; the point is that I began to see that the system was flawed. My understanding was flawed. Things no longer fit neatly in the places where I had kept them stowed. I was wrong.

I was learning that I had placed my faith in a particular theological system rather than in God. I've had to learn that over and over and over again.

That system, as is any, was reckoned on the steady march of precepts, one following and dependent upon the other, girded by supportive interpretation and arguments. If any precept fell out of line, it put at risk the others. You know those people who insist that if you don't believe in a literal six-day creation you won't be able to trust anything the Bible says? Within their system of thinking, they are right!

Biblical anomalies—stories, statements, or perspectives that didn't easily support the fundamental argument the system was designed to prove—had to be ignored or rationalized. And that practice only ever made sense to the ones doing it. For instance, it's still ridiculously obvious to non-Christians that we tend to ignore Jesus's many teachings about legalism and greed, and at the same time rationalize his clear instructions about caring for people who are poor and marginalized by pretending he was talking about us all being spiritually poor. (Until we're saved, anyway.) And people who insist they interpret the Bible literally work and walk unhindered in spite of Jesus's clear instruction, "if your hand or your foot causes you to sin, cut it off and throw it away" (Matt 18:8).

Theological systems tend to treat the Bible as a code book, which, if we unlock its mysteries properly, will provide us with the rules, regulations, and judgments according to which we ought to live. The Bible viewed as "Life's Owners' Manual" is a popular, much reduced expression of this. It's a cute notion, but a problematic analogy. I have lots of owner's manuals, but none of the items to which they apply grow or change or improve with age. The language in them is as clear, concise, and unambiguous as possible, but not so in the Bible. And we human beings are created, each one unique, in the image of God—we don't roll off an assembly line. We're *intended* to be different from each other. How much of what I understand is for me, and how much for everyone? How can we be sure that we're decoding it accurately? What commandments were for then and what commandments are for now? How much is cultural context and how much immutable Word?

For instance, how do we rationalize the unchanging character of the God who commanded that adulterers be stoned to death with Jesus forgiving a woman caught in the act? Is the God who either commanded or allowed Joshua to kill everyone in Jericho except Rahab and her family—"both men and women, young and old, oxen, sheep, and donkeys"—the same God of limitless love and grace we worship today? What about his choice of the Israelites as his people throughout the Old Testament and the sudden inclusion of Gentiles in the New? Slaves were okay then and now they're not? What about the biblical posture toward women: patriarchal, complementarian, or egalitarian?

There are systematic theological rationalizations of all the above, but if you're like me, they tend to sound like exactly that: rationalizations. As long as our theological systems treat the Bible as a code book, the rules, regulations, and judgments and even the representations of God we find within it will create the same kind of dissonance I encountered. Here's why:

Every theological system is an attempt to constrain God. Our systems ultimately tend to submit God to our ideas, despite our opposite intention, because they limit him.

He's big. We're little. Any attempt we make to encompass the infinite must fail. In fact, reducing the God of the Universe to precepts and definitions means we will inevitably misunderstand him. When we define a part of the great mystery, we too often convince ourselves that we have defined the whole. There's value in understanding a leaf, but only if we remember that it's not the tree.

Listen, I'm not unaware of my own proclivities in the matter. Despite my early life experience of constrictive theology, and years of battling to escape it, I'm still inclined to want to know what the rules are. As much as anyone, I'd like God to fall in line with all my expectations of him. I want to believe I'm right. And I have some sense of what dangers those desires lead me into.

However, most of us do genuinely want to understand as much as we can of the Creator. Theological systems are, in their flawed way, attempts to do just that, and have helped us comprehend much of value—even while, in other ways, misleading us. We want to keep learning, not throw up our arms in despair, wailing, "He's unknowable!" God himself makes it evident throughout Scripture and in the created world around us that he desires to be known.

So is there a paradigm shift that could help us see more clearly and go farther?

If it's not a code book or a manual, let me suggest that the Bible is better understood as a story. The greatest story ever told. I'd call it "The Story of God's Redeeming Love."

That's hardly a shocker, is it? This—the concept of what some would call a "narrative theology"—is hardly a new idea. It doesn't mean viewing the Bible as fiction. It means that the biblical story in its entirety is what gives the precepts—the commands and statements within it—their proper meaning, rather than the reverse.

Here's a very clear example. John states a precept: "God is love" (1 John 4:8 and again in 4:16). Then he goes on immediately to tell the story, in very concise fashion, that gives such precious meaning to the precept:

> In this the love of God was made manifest among us, that God sent his only Son into the world, so that we might live through him. In this is love, not that we have loved God but that he loved us and sent his Son to be the propitiation for our sins. (1 John 4:9, 10)

Think about the way you understand a story you read in a book or see on a screen. Even that rare one told from start to finish in straightforward fashion, without flashbacks or flash-forwards, is full of twists and turns, bits you thought you understood and later found you didn't. Some developments you could see coming and some you couldn't. The story is going somewhere, and unless it's some horrifying dystopian mind-bender, it doesn't end up where it started. Once you've arrived at the end, much that was mysterious has become clearer—reading or watching a second time, you find yourself thinking, "Oh, now I get why that happened," or "How did I not see that was important the first time through?"

The ending dictates how we understand the rest of the story.

In systems, anomalies are difficulties that must be rationalized to fit; hence different conclusions from scholars approaching a single anomaly from different paradigms. In a story, anomalies are to be expected and even valued, despite being perhaps in opposition to the "message." In fact, they provide a necessary counterpoint to the story's ending, often depicting a difficulty overcome, a change of perspective, or the growth of an important character. The juxtaposed "wrong" highlights the "right." Evils and obstacles are there to be overcome; if the hero arrives at the end of the story unchanged from the beginning, it's not much of a tale. And, frankly, it's not much like the world we live in. It's the evils and obstacles as much as the good stuff that changes us.

A story has an arc to it, a trajectory that encompasses but ultimately transcends the details within. It lands where it's supposed to—that's what the story is about. The Story of God's Redeeming Love lands where it's supposed to, despite the apparently God-ordained legalism, racial and gender discrimination, and even genocide within it. My own little story is only a miniscule subplot in the great saga, but I trust the Author that it will end as she intends.

By the time that I was walking along that busy road to Quarr, I had already been increasingly inclined toward viewing the biblical account and theology in general from a narrative perspective for some years. That little glimpse of the story's ending—the eternal city coming down out of heaven, like a bride dressed for her husband—was so familiar to me, but now it began working me back through the story in a new way. I had an inkling that my old, default approach still directed my thinking more than I had realized. Those problematic "prohibitive" passages were evidence of that—I had viewed them as precepts to be resolved in themselves, instead of as elements in a larger story. When I couldn't do so definitively, couldn't rationalize them as some did in one direction or the other, I took the other course, setting them aside.

Worse, my approach to the Genesis account of the creation of man and woman amounted to trying to understand the whole story by the way it began instead of by the way it ended. No story—or life!—works that way; present realities shift as what was future becomes present. Things change. Trusting the story required me to submit to God in faith—I might not know how or when we'd get there, but I knew where the story was headed. I'd been reading it over and over since I was a child. Now I needed to take a step back and try to look at the narrative as a whole. Here's what I saw:

I was stuck in the Garden when I was supposed to be headed for the City.

12

The Redemptive Arc

I THINK MOST SERIOUS readers of the Bible would agree that the story it tells has a redemptive arc. The narrative certainly contains substantial elements of gore, judgment and oppression, sometimes apparently sanctioned by God, but where it's headed is just as certainly toward redemption. In fact, the story of redemption responds to and even needs those very sinful, broken elements in order to be a redemption story at all. It's no accident that, for instance, Moses and David were murderers who later became God's men for the moment, or that Peter, the one disciple who explicitly denied Christ at his crucifixion, was the one tapped to be the leading figure in the nascent church. Those specific episodes are in microcosm what the entire story is about.

The concept of a redemptive arc is a familiar one to writers of every kind, but maybe especially screenwriters. In fact, the story of a protagonist who does something bad and, after being refined by trial and overcoming obstacles, makes up for it by doing something really good might just be the most common story arc there is. It's probably a popular form in large part because our Western world has been shaped by the stories of the Bible—redemption stories are familiar to us, and they give us hope when times are hard that things can get better. The difference between the secular and Christian versions of the redemptive arc is that in the one, the hero usually redeems him or herself, and in the biblical saga, it's the hero—Jesus!—who redeems us.

A theologian named William Webb published a book called *Women, Slaves and Homosexuals* in 2001 (InterVarsity) in which he posited an interpretive framework he called a "redemptive movement hermeneutic." Although this framework supposed a biblical trend toward redemption, it didn't take into account how knowing that redemption "ending" might influence our retrospective understanding of the story as a whole. It also supplied a number of subsidiary interpretive "rules" that in practice systematized his hermeneutic and so excluded wider interpretation. Using this system of interpretation, his conclusion was that slaves should definitely be free; women should probably be equal, but there was room for debate; and it was still not okay to be gay.

When I first read his book shortly after its release, I found his structures flawed and inconsistent in themselves. I thought he'd got some of his historical facts wrong, especially about the nature and context of same-gender sexuality in the ancient world. The "slaves, yes; women, maybe; homosexuals, no" result seemed predictable and frankly arbitrary; ultimately it seemed like an elaborate rationalization of the status quo in the conservative world in which Webb had his being. (I wasn't alone in this; I discovered later that a number of scholarly reviewers offered the same criticisms.) Rather than confirming my views at the time, the book left me even more unsettled about their validity.

When I read the book again in preparation for working on this book, another realization about Webb's construct struck me: it just wasn't very redemptive. Yes, it got us to a place that was better than Old Testament times, but that's a pretty low bar. God can redeem this, but not that? Some but not all? I had a feeling God might respond, "Is my hand shortened that it cannot redeem? Or have I no power to deliver?" (Isa 50:2)

It was too caught in the minutiae, too concerned about each step and not enough about the journey's destination. It seemed like yet another case of a system of interpretation "limiting" God's capacity. As Paul wrote, "In him we have redemption through his blood, the forgiveness of our trespasses, according to the riches of his grace, which he lavished upon us, in all wisdom and insight" (Eph 1:7, 8). "Lavished." Not "limited."

Let me declare myself: I believe there is nothing and no one beyond God's power to redeem, nor beyond his desire to do so.

I'm not a historian, but I knew that the first activists for the abolition of the slave trade were Quakers and Anglicans compelled by their faith. William Wilberforce, who drove the issue to its legal culmination in Britain, was not only an abolitionist campaigner, but an evangelical reformer. John Newton, who supported him, was famously a converted slaver, an Anglican minister, and the composer of perhaps still the most widely performed piece of music in history: the hymn "Amazing Grace." Behind these men and others like them were ranks of women who, although they were denied access to government, out of Christian faith gave their money and time to lobby efforts. Many of them sported the famous Josiah Wedgwood medallion depicting a black man in chains, surrounded by the words "Am I Not a Man and a Brother?" In the United States, Frederick Douglass, himself a former slave, declared his devotion to the Christ of the Gospels while castigating the hypocrisy of "Christians" who used Scripture to justify enslaving their brothers. Harriet Tubman, the great hero of the Underground Railroad and later a suffragist, was a devout Christian so conscious of the biblical redemption narrative that she adopted the code name "Moses."

The immorality, the ungodliness of slavery seems so obvious to us now. But there are dozens of passages in the Bible that, at the very least, accept slavery as a societal norm. One even allows for a man to sell his daughter into slavery! (See Exod 21:7.) The closest Scripture ever gets to explicitly advocating for abolition is found in Paul's gentle urging of Philemon to regard Onesimus—Philemon's runaway slave, who, upon his conversion, Paul himself had sent back to his owner—"no longer as a bondservant [slave] but more than a bondservant, as a beloved brother" (Phlm 16). Who would not set an enslaved brother free? Paul implies it—but he doesn't actually say it.

Tacit biblical support for slavery is more common by an order of magnitude than reprobation for same-gender sexuality, yet Christians were at the forefront of the legal eradication of the one, even as some of us continue to dig in our heels on the other. Wilberforce and the others did not set aside Scripture in order to conclude slavery was wrong. They understood that the redemptive agenda within it required going beyond the oppression that had been allowed in the past. They knew that the great story's redemptive arc would land them one day in the New Jerusalem, where all oppression would cease, and every distinction of social condition would be eradicated. If in that day, black people would be their brothers and sisters, their equals in every regard, how in the name of Christ could they enslave them now? The very thought was absurd, the action evil.

You know who else knew it? The slaves themselves. Slave owners went to great lengths to indoctrinate them with a perverse version of Christianity that would keep them subservient, believing that their slavery was sanctioned by God. Nevertheless, as Baylor University professor Robert Darden shows clearly in his books about early black gospel music (*People Get Ready*, Continuum, 2004; *Nothing but Love in God's Water*, Penn State University Press, 2014), the slaves had a better understanding of the justice of God's kingdom and their own place within it than their masters. Ironically, the slaves' oppression set them free to interpret the story in a way that slave owners couldn't, since the owners had to find a way to justify their oppressive position. Long before Martin Luther King Jr. articulated it, those slaves recognized that the "moral arc of the universe is long, but it bends toward justice." We might also expect it, in God's economy, to bend toward reconciliation and unity.

The battle for the equality of women, highlighted early on by the suffragist movement, was similar in that it was fought not only in society at large, but on the ground of differing interpretations of Scripture. Many of those first-wave feminists were at the very least sustained by their Christian faith, if not also directed by it. I doubt anybody would claim Mary Wollstonecraft was a Christian, but people like Maude Royden, a founding member of the Church

League for Women's Suffrage, and Hatty Baker, a trailblazing preacher in the Congregational Church in England, and a founder of Free Church League for Women's Suffrage, certainly were. A Miss L. E. Turquand complained in a letter published in the *Christian Commonwealth* (July 13, 1910) that the conventional church left the suffragists "no place, except in an alien church, where we can bring our movement in touch with religion. Nowhere in our own body can we receive the joy and inspiration, and calm, and consecration which come from lifting a cause into the presence of God."

In spite of biblical arguments mounted against them—and, as with slavery, there are a great many passages that read on the surface as supportive of the subjugation of women—these bold and tenacious women, supported by a small handful of male clergy, fought not only for the right to vote but for equality within the church and society at large. Why were they able to do this still motivated by Christian faith? For some it may have been an intuitive understanding, but for others it must certainly have been a careful exegesis of the biblical narrative and passages summed up in Paul's declaration that "there is no male and female, for you are all one in Christ Jesus" that drove their cause. They understood that the pronouncement of God in Genesis, that Eve's "desire shall be contrary to your husband, but he shall rule over you," was direly prophetic of the results of Adam and Eve's disobedience rather than a statement of God's intention for the fulfilment of humanity.

Redemption, it bears repeating, does not return us to the Garden, but carries us onward to the City. Both the abolitionists and the suffragists knew that Jesus called them to live toward the coming glorious reality, not bound by the sinful oppression of their past and present world.

The issues of slaves, women, and queer folk admittedly have their differences. Slavery during biblical times was a matter of social condition, the result of poverty or being defeated in war, ratified by legal structures. Womanhood was considered at the time to be a matter of physical identity, unchosen and unchangeable, that forever restricted a woman's options and essential value because of societal norms. In the former case, a human being's identity was

altered by his or her social condition; in the latter, a human being's
social condition was determined by her physiology. Neither, however, were to be denied entry into the kingdom of God because of
either their physiology or social condition—in fact, God's redemptive agenda meant that, within that kingdom, slaves and women
have the same status and essential identity as everyone else.

I was long past the point where I could believe, as I once had,
that same-gender attraction or transgender identity were "lifestyle" choices. Increasingly, scientific studies were proving what I
had already concluded: these were matters of core identity, determined by neurological and physiological factors, not choice. And
I realized, the longer I thought about what I had said to BA and
other queer friends since then, that no matter how I protested that
my brokenness was equal to theirs and they were just as beloved of
God as anyone else, my hang-up about same-gender marriage still
relegated them to the position of second-class citizens—as did,
in most cases, the barriers to participation in churches that were
"welcoming" but not "affirming."

Slaves and women wouldn't be second-class in the kingdom
of God. From what I understood, nobody would be. I wouldn't
think of endorsing slavery or the subjugation of women on the
basis that fulfillment of the kingdom was yet to come. I knew I
was supposed to live in the light of that coming reality, live it to
the best of my ability as if it were true already, seeking the necessary changes in both my interior and exterior worlds to bring
them more nearly in line with God's agenda for complete, glorious
redemption. Surely this must be true for my queer friends, as well.

Should we not follow the example of the faithful "strangers
and exiles" of the Old Testament? They wandered because, as the
writer of Hebrews puts it, "they desire a better country, that is a
heavenly one. Therefore God is not ashamed to be called their
God, for he has prepared for them a city" (11:16). I too wanted "a
better country." I wondered if my insistence on remaining in the
Garden—living down to the values of a broken world, instead of up
to those of God's kingdom—might mean that God was ashamed to
be called my God. Sobering thought.

Both Paul's declaration of the ultimate goal of God's redemptive agenda, and John's vision of it, provided a way past the hurdle that had held me up so long—they finally shoved me out of the Garden and set me on a path for the City.

13

That Surprising Ending Gives Clarity

I REALIZED THAT, IF I was reading the story faithfully, along with the expected anomalies and divergent subplots I should be able to find my clarified understanding of the ending foreshadowed earlier in the tale. No story, whether fictional or historical, arrives randomly at its conclusion.

Consider a movie you've seen or a book you've read, one with a killer twist at the ending. Your initial reaction when the lights go up or you slap the cover shut might be something like, "What? How . . . ??" but when the revelation settles in, you think, "Of course!" Because that surprising ending gives clarity to many of the little mysteries you set aside earlier in the story. You may even have thought the story was headed somewhere entirely different, but when it comes to its resolution, you realize how much better the real ending is.

And you can see now that the writer dropped clues all the way along, clues you failed to interpret properly the first time through because you thought the arc would land elsewhere. The literary term for it is foreshadowing. The Bible is full of it, often in ways that are hardly dramatic, since sometimes later passages explicitly unpack the earlier ones.

Example: Jesus is the Lamb of God who takes away the sin of the world (John 1:29). John the Baptist's proclamation was an interpretation of all those passages in the law of Moses that required the sacrifice of a lamb, and before that, the accounts of the first Passover, and earlier still, the ram supplied to die in the place of Isaac when Abraham was about to sacrifice him.

It's worth pointing out that Abraham and Moses didn't know that the lambs they sacrificed foreshadowed the death of God incarnate for the redemption of all creation, nor did the many generations that continued to offer sacrifice in the tabernacle then temple. Such a thought would have been outlandish to them, almost beyond imagination. Characters in a story—whether fiction or nonfiction—can't be expected to know where the story is headed.

I was pretty sure, then, that if the seedling thought that gender distinctions would be wiped out in the City and the goal of the redemptive agenda was "you are all one," I should be able to find clues to that effect throughout the story. Since this was a real story, and people of one generation progressed in their understanding from that of the generation before within it, I thought I could probably expect to find more foreshadowing later than earlier.

One of the first things that became apparent was that the Adam and Eve creation story which had been such a stumbling block for me actually offered some foreshadowing of the very different scene at the end of the Revelation.

"They shall become one flesh," the storyteller says of Man and Woman, expressing the intent of their Creator (Gen 2:24). Paul repeatedly describes the followers of Jesus as one body (Rom 12:5) and the body of Christ (1 Cor 12:27)—and since Jesus was a man, metaphorically that would identify all of us as male. And look, there in Revelation 21: one bride! All redeemed humanity in one flesh. Man, the original human creation, would become (again, metaphorically) by the end of the story Woman. The Creator will not just fix all the ills he prophesied in what is commonly (and mistakenly) called "the Curse" of Genesis 3:16–19, but redeem them, transforming them and us into a radically new and far better reality than original creation. All redeemed men and women as one beautiful bride.

About "the Curse": God cursed the serpent, but not humanity. To Adam and Eve, he only explained what natural consequences would derive from their transgression. The story is descriptive (it tells us what will happen) rather than prescriptive (telling us what should happen). To justify the subjugation of women thereby is to ratify the effects of sin in our world, rather than living in faithful expectation of the ultimate fulfillment of the redemption that is at work in us even now. How did we ever come to think that we should uphold the effects of sin rather than live in and toward redemption?

So, I could now see, the Genesis joining together of man and woman as an expression of the fullness of God in humanity needn't prohibit the joining together of two of the same gender—it could be viewed as a foreshadowing of the story's grand finale, when gender is set aside and all human men and women would be joined as one bride to Christ himself.

It was encouraging to find such clear foreshadowing of the ending—two genders become one, difference becomes unity—right at the start. But surely, if I was headed in the right direction, there would be more.

Oddly enough, revisiting the story of the destruction of Sodom and Gomorrah with a new paradigm was helpful, too. After promising to bless Abraham with children, the Lord (visiting in the form of a man) mentions that he's going to go down to the twin cities on the plain below to have a look around, "because the outcry against Sodom and Gomorrah is great and their sin is very grave" (Gen 18:20). What he finds, of course, leaves him determined to utterly destroy not only the cities, but everything and everyone in them. So, pretty serious then.

Serious indeed. And yet, reading the story now without the presumption that man-on-man sex was the problem left me with a very different perspective on what the sin that so grieved the Lord was. For starters, the account of "the men of Sodom, both young and old, all the people to the last man" surrounding Lot's house and demanding to rape two visitors was clearly intended as an act of violent domination and humiliation, perhaps murder, that bore no resemblance at all to the intimacy, tenderness, and commitment the sexual act is intended to express. This is always the character of rape, regardless of gender; straight men still rape other men in prisons and theaters of war for the same reasons. It seemed evident to me that the men of Sodom would have acted exactly the same way had the two visitors been female. The later, very similar story in which a man's female concubine is the victim seemed to affirm that (Judg 19). In both stories, the gang wanted the men, not because they were attracted to them, but because they hated and perhaps feared them. And in a further heart-breaking twist that shows just how badly broken human valuing of gender and sexual identity is, both gangs were offered women.

I felt like my view of the Sodom story was now much more in line with God's. Ezekiel, as I had already learned, had recorded the Lord's direct judgment on the matter:

> Behold, this was the guilt of your sister Sodom: she and her daughters had pride, excess of food, and prosperous ease, but did not aid the poor and needy. They were haughty and did an abomination before me. So I removed them, when I saw it. (Ezek 16:49, 50)

So then, haughty pride and a failure to care for the poor and needy were the substance of the outcry the Lord heard and went to investigate. The vicious, abominable intent of the men of Sodom (whose city, ironically, is characterized here as female) toward the two visitors derived directly from that attitude. It made me wonder if the two men had showed up looking like homeless vagrants. For all his faults, Lot's behavior was, at least initially, in this instance righteous, and counter to the charges of Ezekiel—he welcomed the visitors lavishly, insisted they not stay in the town square, where he knew they'd be vulnerable, but took them into his own house, made them a feast and protected them against the mob (Gen 19:1–8; he offered the Sodomites his daughters, too, which beggars belief and, obviously, was far from a righteous thing to do).

There was nothing all that new to me in these conclusions so far. On the other hand, even Jude's comment about the people of the twin cities having "indulged in sexual immorality and pursued unnatural desire" didn't now sound like a condemnation of gay sex specifically, but of sexual immorality in general (sex as an activity, without fidelity or relationship) and sex pursued as acts of domination and abuse rather than intimate love (Jude 7). There was nothing "natural," in the good sense of the word, in the desire of the mob to rape a couple of innocent visitors to their town. There was, still, no affirmation of same-gender relationship inherent in either the Genesis account or the Ezekiel commentary.

The big reveal was this: if God so hated homosexual behavior, wouldn't this have been the ideal opportunity to say so? Wouldn't he have added a phrase to the judgment Ezekiel had recorded to make it clear that "abomination" meant or at least included gay sex? Something like, "Plus they wanted to have man-on-man sex, which is *disgusting!* Wrong! That's why I burned the place to the ground."

But he didn't say that. Didn't say anything about it. *It seems it was irrelevant to God.* And again I thought, "Well, gender will apparently be irrelevant when we're 'in the bride.' So that fits."

I reviewed the stories of Ruth and Naomi, and David and Jonathan, which some apologists liked to assert were lightly cloaked accounts of same-gender romantic love. They pointed out that when it says Ruth "clung" to Naomi, it's the same Hebrew word used to describe the way a man will "hold fast" to his wife in Genesis 2:24. Furthermore, they'd observe, Ruth's declaration that "where you go I will go, where you lodge I will lodge" (Ruth 1:16) has, from ancient times, been a part of traditional Hebrew wedding ceremonies and even some Christian ones. That, it seemed to me, was arguing backwards, but it was certainly a remarkable statement.

Ruth actually wanted to die where Naomi, the much older woman, would die (1:17). She clearly loved her very, very much and intended to commit herself to the relationship for life. It was interesting, and might be a dim reflection, but it was hardly conclusive—in the context, it didn't seem to point with any great clarity to Christ's union with his bride, especially as Ruth went on to marry a man, Boaz. On the other hand, Ruth wasn't just an obscure OT character—against the conventions of the day, she'd make it into Matthew's genealogy of Jesus. So, it seemed, her story was of particular significance. And, I realized, there was also no social context at all at that time that would have allowed the two women to marry if they'd wanted to, and they did remain very close—when Ruth bore Boaz a child, the neighborhood women said, "A son has been born to Naomi" (Ruth 4:17). There's certainly not a whiff of approbation of what is at least a deeply intimate, life-long emotional relationship in the passage. If they'd actually had a sexual relationship, it occurred to me, it would not have been prohibited by the law of Moses. So, hmm. . . . A hint, maybe, a pos-sibility, but so inconclusive as to be irrelevant to my search.

Revisiting the story of David and Jonathan was more interest-ing. Perhaps there was more to it than I had thought. After the young David had defeated Goliath, and was presented to King Saul, the king's son Jonathan

> loved him as his own soul. And Saul took him that day and would not let him return to his father's house. Then Jonathan made a covenant with David, because he loved him as his own soul. And Jonathan stripped himself of the robe that was on him and gave it to David, and his armour, and even his sword and his bow and his belt.
> (1 Sam 18:1–4)

The Hebrew word accurately translated "loved" sometimes refers to friend-love, but more frequently to lovers. Okay . . . and what was the nature of the covenant they made? Again, the word is applied in the Bible to treaties between peoples, and to pledges made by servants of one kind or another to their lord, but also to marriage. It's the word most commonly used to describe God's covenant commitment to his people. The covenant that will ulti-mately be fulfilled at the Marriage Supper of the Lamb.

Pretty strong term, then. Jonathan's removal of his armor, weapons, and robe and his gift of them to David made it clear that this was about more than just liking the guy. Maybe it was a way of recognizing the great victory David had won for Israel and Jonathan's father the king. But it did seem like a radical en-actment of making oneself vulnerable. I thought some of the gay commentators I read made a reasonable point when they claimed that, had David been a woman, every reader encountering this scene would immediately recognized this as a love story.

That view seemed, possibly, to be borne out by the many proclamations of love between the two as the story unfolded, and by the narrator's repeated observation that Jonathan "loved him as he loved his own soul" (1 Sam 20:17). A pretty strong phrase, that one.

Later, David would declare before the people of Judah, in a song he had written to eulogize both Saul and Jonathan following their deaths in battle, "I am distressed for you, my brother Jonathan; very pleasant have you been to me; your love to me was extraordinary, surpassing the love of women" (2 Sam 1:26). "Pleasant" might just mean David had enjoyed hanging out with Jonathan, but the word sometimes meant "physically attractive," in the same way the bridegroom depicts his bride in the Song of Solomon 7:6: "How beautiful and pleasant you are, O loved one, with all your delights!" In that passage at least, there was no mistaking Solomon's erotic intention. (Read a little farther down in that chapter. Gets positively steamy.)

Hm. Maybe just the hyperbole of a young man distraught at the death of his best bud, his "brother." But there was also something else, earlier in the story. Not long after David killed Goliath, King Saul had become resentful and afraid of the young hero. At the supper table one night, when Jonathan attempted to run interference for his beloved David, Saul erupted at his son: "You son of a perverse, rebellious woman, do I not know that you have chosen the son of Jesse to your shame, and to the shame of your mother's nakedness?" (1 Sam 20:30.) He went on to threaten David's life, and when Jonathan asked why David deserved to die, chucked a spear at his own son.

I had never considered Saul's accusation carefully before. It could simply be that Saul was angry because he perceived Jonathan as having shifted his allegiance from Saul, and even from his own heritage, to David. Yet he said explicitly that he regarded the relationship as shameful. Why? He was certainly worried that

David was more popular with his subjects than he was himself. But it intrigued me that Saul also blamed Jonathan's mother, and accused Jonathan of shaming her nakedness. "Nakedness," I knew, was a biblical euphemism for sexual shame. And it's practically a tradition for a square-headed dad to blame mom for producing a gay son. Whether or not that's actually what was going on with the two young men, Saul seemed to be accusing them of a romantic relationship.

Saul's anger, while it seems to have been driven by jealousy and fear, was also in line with those passages in the law that required a death sentence for a man lying with a man as he would with a woman. It seems unlikely that David and Jonathan would have flouted that law, unless by that period in history there was a common understanding that it was to be understood as referring to a specific social/religious context limited to the time of Moses. Possible. Far from certain. And would both the prophet Samuel and the Apostle Paul have called David a man after God's heart (1 Sam 13:14; Acts 13:22) if they thought that's what the two men had been doing? On the other hand, David was a murderer and adulterer, too. That hadn't stopped them.

The story of David and Jonathan is often touted as a beautiful example of deep, godly, intimate, and completely platonic friendship. Maybe that's exactly what it was. David, after all, would go on to marry several women, have a whack of kids and prove himself such a hetero lecher that he'd murder Uriah just to get his hooks on Bathsheba. Maybe it was nothing, but maybe there was something there. Never would David declare his love for a woman the way he and Jonathan had to each other.

Maybe it was nothing. But foreshadowing is rarely clear and definitive; it's usually just a hint. Maybe it was a whisper, a rumor of where the Story of God's Redeeming Love was headed.

14

Bent to the Inclusion of Every Outsider

I DIDN'T FIND ANYTHING else in the Old Testament that I thought
might foreshadow the landing place of the redemptive arc as re-
gards queer folk. Nor was there anything that condemned committed, loving relationship between equal partners. There was that
gruesome passage in Judges 19 that echoed the Sodom account,
except that it was a woman who was ultimately gang-raped by men
of the town (which, as I've already pointed out, supports the idea
that the Sodomites were bent on violent domination, not gay sex).
Several passages in 1 and 2 Kings referred to the presence of cultic
male prostitutes in the governments of apostate kings—along with
other forms of infidelity—but that was as contrary to the biblical
vision I was pursuing as my own attraction to anonymous prostitutes had been to the marital relationship that was (and once again
is, I'm happy to say) my heart's truest, God-directed desire.

As with the Ezekiel judgment, I found the silence intriguing. Same-gender sexual activity was, from what I'd read, fairly
common in the cultures that surrounded the Israelite nation,
especially as a feature of cult religion. Yahweh was certainly not
sparing in his condemnation of others of those nations' activities, and the apostasies into which they frequently tempted the
Israelites, but he didn't seem inclined to single out same-gender
sexuality for judgment. In fact, apostasy was most frequently

characterized in the prophetic books as spiritual adultery, a betrayal of the "marriage bond" between God and his people—clearly heterosexual metaphors.

It wasn't "affirming"; it just seemed like it wasn't really on God's radar. Mind you, there wasn't much that gave definitive hope of across-the-board emancipation to women or slaves, either. The best that could be said was that Mosaic laws appeared to have been a little more humane in that regard than those of surrounding nations.

On the other hand, the surprising rise of Aaron's sister Miriam as national worship leader and prophetess, and Deborah as the lone female judge, as well as prophetess and military leader, did seem to offer a hint of something better to come. And of course, there was a steady current of verses and passages indicating God's intention to welcome, give sustenance to, and even integrate people who were unimportant or whom a "good" Israelite might otherwise be inclined to exclude: widows, orphans, foreigners. God's choice of the unimportant wanderer, Abraham, as the father of his chosen people, was an expression of that theme; his choice again of a rootless nation of slaves, his deliverance of them, and their eventual establishment in a country of their own, was at the root of perhaps the most compelling narrative of the entire Old Testament.

The prophetic books were rife with that intention to bring in the excluded and raise up the oppressed. I thought the expression of it reached its apex in Isaiah 61, the passage the Jesus himself would choose as his mission statement:

> The Spirit of the Lord GOD is upon me,
> because the LORD has anointed me
> to bring good news to the poor;
> he has sent me to bind up the broken-hearted,
> to proclaim liberty to the captives,
> and the opening of the prison to those who are bound;
> to proclaim the year of the LORD's favour.
> (vv. 1, 2)

Not only would these discarded people be welcomed, but, the prophet went on to declare, it was people who were poor, captives, blind, and oppressed (according to the version quoted in Luke 4) who would be the very ones right at the heart of a redeemed kingdom:

> They shall build up the ancient ruins;
> they shall raise up the former devastations;
> they shall repair the ruined cities,
> the devastations of many generations.
> Strangers shall stand and tend your flocks;
> foreigners shall be your plowmen and vinedressers;
> but you shall be called the priests of the Lord;
> they shall speak of you as the ministers of our God;
> you shall eat the wealth of the nations,
> and in their glory you shall boast.
> Instead of your shame there shall be a double portion;
> instead of dishonor they shall rejoice in their lot;
> therefore in their land they shall possess a double portion;
> they shall have everlasting joy.
> (Isa 61:4–7)

The very people who had been shamed would be given a "double portion"—an expression of honor—and "everlasting joy." I thought again of those men on the Steps, desolate and hopeless in their shame, and Roxanne, dying alone and rejected by her family. Cassandra, beaten to death by an irate trick. Didn't they fit here?

The honoring of the shamed and the inclusion of the rejected was, I realized, apparent in the very first verses of the New Testament—right there in the very lineage of Jesus Christ, Son of David, Son of Abraham.

Matthew's genealogy of the Messiah started off with Abraham himself, of course, the unremarkable wanderer who God tapped to be the most famous and widely-claimed "father" of peoples in history. A couple of counterintuitive second sons, Jacob and Judah, in an age of primogeniture, selected in the same way. And most remarkably, Matthew goes out of his way to mention four scandalous mothers in a list that typically wouldn't have included women at all.

Tamar, a victim of incest who sought justice by disguising herself as a prostitute and entrapping her domineering father-in-law,

Judah. Nasty piece of work, Judah. Tough, resilient, and morally, um, pragmatic woman, that Tamar.

Rahab, a foreigner, citizen of a city to be utterly destroyed by God's people; oh, and a prostitute. Salman must have been a gutsy guy marrying her, given the way most Israelites likely viewed her.

Good old Ruth, another foreigner, a widow, who literally threw herself at the feet of Boaz.

Bathsheba, pointedly described as "the wife of Uriah," who David murdered. The spoils of a personal war. And as Uriah was a Hittite, a member of an ethnic minority living in Israel at the time, it seems likely that Bathsheba was, too. Another foreigner, then. Outsiders all.

David himself is of course the pivotal figure, since it was as the "Son of David" that Jesus would be acclaimed Messiah. He started out as the overlooked youngest son, loved Jonathan, and was loved by him intensely, was hunted and driven into exile for years, and finally became king. Classic outsider. His behavior as king was pretty spotty—arranging the murder of one of his captains so that he could possess a woman who had no say in the matter whatsoever; his nepotism driving the nation into civil war. And Solomon was the issue of that nefarious union, the famous Solomon, a paragon of wisdom and poetry until he started thinking with his nether regions and collecting practically every woman within reach.

Even Jesus was born of a young woman whose supposed morals, though she was innocent, must have been the subject of many a salacious whisper.

Clearly, it would be a stretch to say that any of this constituted a positive statement that "queer is good." But the story consistently points in one direction. The fact that the human lineage of the Christ, the Son of the Living God, took so many unexpected twists and turns, and included so many who might understandably be expected to be excluded by the steady march through history of God's righteous precepts, was a powerful reminder:

God's righteousness is bent to the inclusion of every outsider, the redemption of every sinner, and striking off the chains of every oppressive system.

It was becoming clear to me that the redemption of queer people, however that was to be effected, was just one strand of the whole grand sweep of the Story of God's Redeeming Love. If part of the point of the Great Consummation was the reconciling of all into one, then it made sense to me that God's attitude to one kind of people in need of redemption was the same as his attitude to all the others. His inclusion of anyone who was excluded was the story of his inclusion of everyone.

Nobody is beyond God's reach or his intention. God's judgment is not for the purpose of putting distance between us and him, but for eradicating everything than stands between us. Instead of standing back and holding his nose at our sin, he said (in effect), "Grrr! I hate this stuff that keeps us apart!" And then he destroyed it. All of the men and women in that list were functioning sinners and victims of the sins of others, some of them extravagantly so. Just like me. Just like my queer friends. "There is no distinction," Paul concludes his lengthy description of the utter brokenness of humanity, "all have sinned and come short of the glory of God, and are justified by his grace as a gift, through the redemption that is in Christ Jesus" (Rom 3:23, 24).

God's intention, which will surely be accomplished, is to reconcile all of us into one body and present us as a bride, "in splendor, without spot or wrinkle or any such thing," to his Son (Eph 5:27). A puzzle for most men, to be sure, not to mention bisexual, asexual, and nonbinary people, but that's the climax of the redemption story. I kept thinking, "Shouldn't we be doing our best to live that ultimate reality here and now?"

"It is not the will of my Father who is in heaven that one of these little ones should perish," Jesus told his disciples (Matt 18:14). They had asked who would be most important in the coming kingdom. Jesus's surprising answer was that it was whoever would become childlike—humble, dependent on their heavenly parents, vulnerable. Receiving them was the same as receiving him, he said. Then he offered this frightening warning:

> Whoever causes one of these little ones who believe in me to sin, it would be better for him to have a great millstone fastened around his neck and to be drowned in the sea. (Matt 18:6)

Uh oh. Once again, I couldn't help but think of all the queer folk I knew who had been driven away from Christian faith, or had been convinced that they were excluded to start with, by the actions and words of Christian people.

One of the beautiful things about children, especially really little ones, is that they don't question who they are. They don't think about whether or not they are pretty or smart or morally right. They don't ask themselves or others, "Is it okay to be me?" They just are. They don't expect to have to change who they are in order to be acceptable. My five-year-old granddaughter Branna never even questions whether or not she is acceptable. She is, of course, far more than merely acceptable; she's beloved. She swims in love as unconscious of it as a fish is of water. I think that's the kind of picture Jesus was drawing.

And so I had to wonder: if being queer is a matter of who you are, not just your actions, what would Jesus expect of an LGTBQ2+ person who came to him like a child? Would it be the denial of selfishness, pride, and the many sinful activities which spring from them, plus the positive actions of practical discipleship, to which he called all of us? I thought so. But did he require also a denial of that which seemed undeniable—a core part of their nature?

I felt convinced that Paul, in his statement of the redemptive agenda in Galatians 3:28, and John, with his depiction of the City/ Bride at the consummation of all things in Revelation 21, gave me a clear sense of where the story would land. Every divisive, hierarchical distinction of ethnicity and culture, of economic standing and social condition, of gender and sexuality would be rendered irrelevant. Together, as one bride, we would be joined to the Son of the Living God.

The Creation account, I now believed, planted a broad hint as to the direction this story was headed, and I thought I could at least detect whispers and echoes here and there throughout the Old Testament that were like stepping-stones on the same wandering path.

The epistles of the New Testament lead us a little farther along the trajectory of that story than the Gospels. But having grown up with an interpretive paradigm that diminished the Gospels, making the life and teaching of Jesus mere reference material for the teaching of Paul and the others, I wanted to defer to Jesus. I wanted to know what he had to say about the issue, and I wanted to have some confidence that I was interpreting Paul and John in the light of it.

The problem was, Jesus didn't say anything specific about same-gender sexuality.

15

Jesus Knew What Was Going On

THE FAMOUS "SERMON ON the Mount" (Matt 5–7) and the subsequent slightly less so "Sermon on the Plain" (Luke 6:20–49) represent Jesus's first big public appearances. Before that, he'd been baptized by John, gathered his disciples, declared his mission in the synagogue of his hometown, and done a little healing here and there. The buzz started to grow. Great crowds started to follow him around, gathering from all over the Jewish territories of Judea and Galilee, as well as from some of the Gentile lands that bordered them. If you conflate the two accounts, it appears that Jesus delivered the Sermon on the Mount, came down into the towns nearby, did some more healing and such, and then preached a similar, more concise and slightly more pointed sermon again on the plain on which the towns sat. Then he went back home to Capernaum.

Most expositors of those sermons—and there have been a ton of them—agree that they are, in essence, the Charter of the Kingdom of God, the distillation of Jesus's most foundational teaching. I have no intention of exegeting them yet again, except to point out that they reaffirm in no uncertain terms God's determination to include, right at the heart of his kingdom, people who are disregarded, diminished, and disposed of everywhere else. Already, by this point, a reader of the gospels has come to expect that Jesus will heal the lepers and the lame, and he doesn't disappoint.

But he does surprise. The man he engaged next, as soon as he'd left the crowds behind and gone home, was about the last person you'd have expected: a centurion of the Roman army. He was undoubtedly a seasoned veteran of the empire's wars, probably entrusted with the command of the occupying force quartered to the east of the town, and most likely wealthy, at least in comparison with the locals. He may not have been Roman at all, but one of Herod's mercenaries from another Gentile nation. Galileans hated Rome and all it stood for—idolatry and oppression, among other sins—but they despised Herod as an imposter and a traitor, a usurper of the throne of David. The centurion represented everything Jewish people of the time distrusted. Even the new adherents to the radical good news preached by Jesus would have expected him to be ineligible for the kingdom of heaven.

Both Matthew (8:5–13) and Luke (7:1–10) tell the story, I believe, precisely because it's so counterintuitive. These two gospels were written later than Mark's, which doesn't include this account. Perhaps it took a while before early Christians could believe it had happened.

The centurion had a slave who was dying. He must have been sensitive to how he might be viewed by this new Jewish firebrand preacher and miracle worker, because Luke says that instead of approaching Jesus directly, he asked the local elders to advocate for him. They did so, pleading in fact, saying that the soldier was a good guy who loved Jewish people and had even paid for the construction of the town's synagogue.

> And Jesus went with them. When he was not far from the house, the centurion sent friends, saying to him, "Lord, do not trouble yourself, for I am not worthy to have you come under my roof. Therefore I did not presume to come to you. But say the word, and let my servant be healed." (from Luke's version of the story)

Jesus was impressed, remarking that "with no one in Israel have I found such faith." He respected the centurion's exceptional humility and didn't continue on to his house but told the soldier's friends to go deliver the message that the slave would be healed. He also offered this commentary, underscoring the way his kingdom would flip the assumption of religious entitlement on its head:

> I tell you, many will come from east and west and recline at table with Abraham, Isaac, and Jacob in the kingdom of heaven, while the sons of the kingdom will be thrown into the outer darkness. In that place there will be weeping and gnashing of teeth. (from Matthew's version)

I knew that Jesus's warning was specifically about Gentiles like the centurion being accepted while some of the Jews who took their place for granted—many of the Pharisees came immediately to mind—would find themselves in the dark. But I thought there was a deeper principle being expressed, too: it reminded me that it was just as dangerous for me to make assumptions about who was "in" and who was "out."

So far, the story as I've related it is surprising because the ones blessed are a figure of idolatry, power, and oppression and the very figure of his opposite: his slave. Oppressor and oppressed, both blessed by the Redeemer in one extravagant action; a dramatic illustration of the radical reconciliation that is the ultimate goal of the gospel.

Some apologists for queer Christian faith take the story even farther, asserting that a closer look reveals that the centurion and his slave were a gay couple.

There are two words used for "slave" (a more accurate translation than "servant") in these passages. One is the usual generic term for a person who is not merely hired but is bound as a servant to another, with no freedom to leave and no power to require payment or evade abuse. Although the culture of the time tended to use the word "master," the centurion was really the "owner" of this slave.

As I've intimated earlier, the second word, the one the centurion himself uses to describe his slave, means "boy." Some scholars say that this term was sometimes used to refer to a male lover, as almost invariably, male same-gender couples in that era involved an older, wealthier man and a younger usually teenaged dependant who either received some advantage financially or socially from the relationship, or who had no real choice in the matter. In fact, it was relatively common in the Greco-Roman world for men to own attractive young male slaves specifically as sexual servants. So, a man might say, "my boy," and mean either "my young slave" or "my young sexual partner." (He might mean, "my son" too, the way some dads still do, although that at least is clearly not the case here.)

There were also other terms used that specifically identified both older and younger men in sexual relationship, and still others referring to their particular physical roles in the act of sex—which were also almost always tied to age and status. (Classical scholar Kenneth Dover published what may still be the definitive text about all this stuff in 1978, plainly titled *Greek Homosexuality*, Harvard University Press. Other scholars have published similar findings, so it's certainly not a matter of relying on fringe opinions to consider this stuff.)

Luke also remarked that the centurion's slave was "highly valued" by him. An interesting term, that. As with the word for "boy," it has a range of meaning: honored, highly valued, precious. The good ol' King James Version translates it here as "dear to him."

Luke used the same word later, quoting Jesus: "When you are invited by someone to a wedding feast, do not sit down in a place of honor, lest someone more *distinguished* than you be invited by him" (14:8).

Paul wrote to the Philippians regarding his messenger, Epaphroditus, "So receive him in the Lord with all joy, and *honor* such men" (2:29).

And Peter would use the same word to refer to Jesus:

> As you come to him, a living stone rejected by men but in the sight of God chosen and *precious*, you yourselves like living stones are being built up as a spiritual house, to be a holy priesthood, to offer spiritual sacrifices acceptable to God through Jesus Christ. (2 Pet 2:4, 5)

The boy-slave was certainly highly valued and regarded by the centurion for some reason. It was hard to imagine a battle-scarred veteran holding a young boy he actually owned in such honor—the term reflected far more than a merely monetary value, although it didn't necessarily carry an explicit sexual or romantic connotation. Remarkable, really, and a detail it seemed to me that Luke's account could have gotten by without, as Matthew's did, unless Luke thought it was important to the overall meaning.

But there were far less ambiguous terms available to Matthew and Luke; if they had wanted to make it clear there was a sexual relationship between the two, wouldn't they have used them? Or did they sense that the concept of the good news extending to a figure of idolatrous Roman oppression was enough for the Christians of their time to grapple with, and so just left the rest in there as a subtle hint that could be read or ignored according to the reader's capacity?

Whatever Matthew's and Luke's take on the story had really been, Jesus likely knew what was going on. Maybe he had blessed a gay couple, as some commentators like to confidently assert. If so, he had offered no word of judgment on their relationship.

Of course, he hadn't challenged the centurion about oppressing the Jewish people or owning a slave, either. He'd just healed the boy and praised the older man's faith, without addressing any of their sins—regardless of what they were. I had to think about this some more.

The relationship of the centurion and his boy, if it was a sexual one, was prototypical for the time. Sexuality was not regarded in binary fashion—either gay or straight—as it often is today. (At least within the church. Elsewhere, that's changing rapidly.) The term "homosexuality" wasn't even coined until, it's thought, sometime in the 1870s, by Karl-Maria Kertbeny, a Hungarian journalist and human rights activist. (He also came up with "heterosexual.") "Pederasty" (boy love) had long described the usual context of male same-gender sexual relationship dating back to the ancients, and the term was redolent with the power discrepancies and consequent abuses that were ubiquitous in such relationships. From what I read, it was rare and not widely acceptable, even in pagan societies, for two men to have an equal, loving, and committed relationship that included sex. (Women seem to have found it much easier to fly under the radar.)

The other main context for same-gender sex was religious cult prostitution—under a variety of religious rubrics, young male priests or acolytes submitted themselves to the sexual acts of male "worshippers," on payment of a donation to the temple.

In either case, it helped me understand that Paul's condemnation of "bed-men" and "effeminates" and people who "exchanged natural relations for those that were contrary to nature" were at least primarily an indictment of abuse, idolatry, sexual adventurism, and infidelity. Although I suspected he wouldn't have been too keen on the nature of the sexual relationship, if there was one, between the centurion and his boy, there was simply no context for him to comment on the sexuality of two people of the same gender who loved each other and committed themselves to each other in marriage, or a similar covenant.

And that brought me back to women and slaves. There was no social context for the equality of women or the culture-wide emancipation of slaves, either. (Individual slaves did, sometimes, manage to purchase their freedom, or were awarded it by an appreciative master.) No wonder Paul, although progressive for his time, still seemed to affirm the continuing subjugation of both— perhaps it wasn't affirmation at all, but pragmatic instruction to people who were living at a particular time within the constraints of a particular culture.

In addressing the social realities of his era, then, I couldn't expect Paul or other New Testament writers to directly confront matters of ethnic, social, or sexual identity inequities. But what would he say was the greater reality of God's plan? What would he say ought to be? Where were we supposed to be headed?

Well, I knew that one already:

> There is neither Jew nor Greek, there is neither slave nor free, there is no male and female, for you are all one in Christ Jesus.

16

Room for "Those People"

HERE'S A DEMOGRAPHIC YOU don't hear much about these days: eunuchs.

If you're an average guy, just the word itself might make you clench a bit. In most of the ancient world, it was common practice to slice off either part (just the testicles) or all of a boy's or young man's tackle. Presumably the wound was cauterized. The process was so gruesome it hardly bears thinking about, and the mortality rate must have been high. Many eunuchs were slaves subjected to this treatment against their will, but surprisingly there were volunteers, too: for a bright or attractive young man who was poor and had no other prospects it could be an excellent career move. So much so that some few apparently even did the surgery on themselves. (Taking a deep breath here, and moving on. . . .)

It was thought that castration made a man less ambitious and more loyal—thus, an excellent servant in a royal court where the king had always to be looking over his shoulder. A eunuch who had been castrated as a boy skipped most of the effects of puberty, retaining smooth, hairless skin and a high-pitched voice that, if he could hold a note, might be valued musically. Some would consider him to be aesthetically pleasing both to look at and listen to, and he certainly would not have seemed at all threatening in the hypermasculine atmosphere of a despot's court. Eunuchs were popular bodyguards for kings; the lack of testosterone didn't preclude them being big, strong, and, once trained, adept with weapons, especially if they'd been castrated after puberty. Because they were often so physically close to the king—guarding him, serving his meals, even dressing and bathing him—these men frequently became trusted advisors and might even be granted official office as such.

They could also be trusted to guard the king's wife, or wives and concubines, whether the women were sequestered in a physical harem, as was sometimes the case in Eastern kingdoms, or were allowed a little more freedom. A man castrated after puberty lost all his power to impregnate the king's women, and much but not necessarily all of his capacity to perform sexually. In some cultures, the king really didn't care much if his women had sex with someone else—it might even help them stave off the boredom of their highly constricted lives—as long as he could be certain that any children born to them were his. A trusty eunuch who accompanied one of the king's women every time she left the security of the harem was an excellent safeguard against her dallying with a more potent man.

Furthermore, the senior wife in the harem—or sometimes the queen mother—was frequently entrusted by the king with the administration of the household treasury. Given that in most ancient kingdoms the king's wealth was the country's wealth, a position in the treasury was akin to one in a modern government's finance ministry. From singing in court entertainments, to general household or security service, all the way up to senior levels of the court's bureaucracy, eunuchs could be found from the most ancient societies through to the fall of Rome.

Jews, however, were a historical and social anomaly in this regard. The law of Moses prohibited bodily mutilation of any sort ("You shall not make any cuts on your body for the dead or tattoo yourselves: I am the LORD," Lev 19:28), and although that statute oddly followed one that provided instructions on haircuts, Jewish people seemed to have obeyed it assiduously. Furthermore, emasculation was specifically and forcefully prohibited on pain of excommunication: "No one whose testicles are crushed or whose male organ is cut off shall enter the assembly of the LORD" (Deut 23:1).

Castration was so anathema to the Hebrews that a Levite who had a damaged testicle, even one damaged by accident, was not allowed to serve in the tabernacle, and an animal in the same condition was excluded as a valid sacrifice (Lev 21:20; 22:24).

The very idea of castration was perhaps even more repellent to observant Jews of Jesus's day than it would be to most of us now. Added to their repugnance at the horrific physical mutilation was the eunuch's subsequent incapacity to produce children, which was considered a moral duty, a financial practicality (more kids meant more income earners for the family), security for mom and dad when they got old, a man's heritage and posterity, and, let's face it, a public statement about the virility of ol' dad. Kids, and lots of them, were considered to be proof-positive of God's blessing:

> Behold, children are a heritage from the LORD,
> the fruit of the womb a reward.
> Like arrows in the hand of a warrior
> are the children of one's youth.
> Blessed is the man
> who fills his quiver with them!
> (Ps 127:3–5)

"Eunuch" was about the most odious characterization of sexual and gender identity that a religious Jewish person in the time of Jesus could imagination. And it was an identity, not just a practice or proclivity, as same-gender sex was then considered to be. Once they'd been sliced off, there was no going back. You were a eunuch, period. You had been desexed, and while certainly not a woman, were not now really a man either.

So why was I considering such grim subject matter at such great length?

Because I'd remembered that Jesus had gone out of his way to talk about them, and in counterculturally positive terms:

> For there are eunuchs who have been so from birth, and there are eunuchs who have been made eunuchs by men, and there are eunuchs who have made themselves eunuchs for the sake of the kingdom of heaven. Let the one who is able to receive this receive it. (Matt 19:12)

Not just one, but three categories of eunuchs! Those who "have been made eunuchs by men" seemed easy enough to identify—they'd be the ones I've just been describing—but who was included in the other two categories?

Well, I supposed, people born without the ability to have kids, or the interest in doing so, might be the first group. That would include intersex people like Roxanne, or people who are asexual. They would be scorned by men like the disciples, too. Queer people are finding ways to have children now, but they couldn't then. I wondered if they were included in Jesus's description.

The middle category would be what most of Jesus's hearers would think of first—the castrated unfortunates common enough in the Greco-Roman world, but anathema to the Jewish mind.

Those "who have made themselves eunuchs for the sake of the kingdom of heaven" had to mean, at the very least, people who chose to (a) avoid having children even while married, or (b) remain celibate entirely in order to serve God better. Paul seems to have been one of those. To call them eunuchs, though, was to identify these godly people with a figure that was both foreign and deeply offensive to the contemporary Jewish mind.

To be crystal clear: he was equating people who chose childlessness or celibacy as an expression of devotion to God with (a) people whose natural orientation or condition of birth meant they'd never have children and (b) people who had been castrated, either by choice or against their will. They had effectively desexed themselves, while avoiding the radical surgery.

Jesus's final comment on the matter, "Let the one who is able to receive this receive it," made it evident that he knew his disciples would struggle to understand and accept what he had said. Some wouldn't get it at all. None of those three options made sense to them. Even if he'd just said, "There are some people who will choose to be celibate for the sake of the kingdom of God," they'd have had a hard time understanding why. Raising the subject of eunuchs in a positive way was nothing short of shocking. Bridging from an earlier conversation (which I'll come back to), he'd begun this surprising statement by saying "Not everyone can receive this saying, but only those to whom it is given" (v. 11) In other words, there's a mystery here to be investigated and worked out.

He chose the sexual identity that his disciples would view as the most extremely "other," and made it clear there was room for "those people" in the kingdom of heaven. It was a clear departure from the deep-rooted values of the disciples' culture and their interpretation of Scripture. He knew it would require a lot of wrestling with both to be able to accept it. A small comfort, that—Jesus understood how slow I would be.

I could see that what he was teaching here was perfectly in line with the gospel he preached and the kingdom he announced, in which the first would be last and the last first. People who were despised and excluded in this world, including eunuchs, would be found right at the heart of the kingdom of heaven. It seemed clear to me that he used the word "eunuch" as a catchall term for everyone whose sexual or gender identity would result in them being regarded as second-class citizens or beyond the boundaries of the kingdom entirely. Because even "eunuchs" aren't despised or excluded by God.

This dissertation of Jesus to his disciples in private represented a hard-left turn from a conversation he'd had with a group of Pharisees in public earlier on. Going back to that part of the story strengthened what I thought he meant about eunuchs—and it was personally convicting, too.

The account began with these religious dogmatists trying out yet another theological challenge on the new young rabbi. Wasn't it true that the law allowed them, the men, to divorce their wives for any reason at all? (See Matt 19:3ff. I'm paraphrasing.) They must have known that he'd offer a perspective divergent from theirs, and—this was the trap—contrary to a societal perspective that was widespread and pretty much set in stone. If Jesus blew this one as they hoped, he'd risk alienating men everywhere.

In any practical terms, it was impossible for a woman to divorce her husband: if she did, she'd be out on the street without protection, income, or status. Moses hadn't even contemplated a woman seeking divorce, and neither did the Pharisees. In fact, the law didn't so much set out clear divorce legislation as create some restrictions for what was evidently already taking place. (See Deut 24:1–4.) Those conditions were aimed at protecting vulnerable women, but the Pharisees, who were so strict about adhering to the minutiae of the law when it served them, interpreted this particular statue to mean that they could freely dispose of a wife simply because it suited them to do so. Because, perhaps, they'd had their eye on a younger, more attractive woman than the one they were already married to.

As they had expected, Jesus bit down hard on the bait. Moses had only written that law in the first place to mitigate their abuse of women, he said. Disposing of one wife for the purpose of marrying another was nothing short of adultery. This was never God's intention. Here's what was:

> Have you not read that he who created them from the beginning made them male and female, and said, "Therefore a man shall leave his father and his mother and hold fast to his wife, and the two shall become one flesh"? So they are no longer two but one flesh. What therefore God has joined together, let not man separate. (vv. 4–6)

Ah. There it was again, repeated twice for emphasis: "the two shall become one flesh." The echo of God's redemptive agenda and the landing place of the redemptive arc of the story. Male and female as one, together joined to Christ. His intention from the very beginning: there are two now, but then they will become only one.

Jesus's emphatic statement that husbands couldn't just do whatever they wanted was so counter to the prevailing view that his disciples responded, "If such is the case of a man with his wife, it is better not to marry." And Jesus went on, saying in effect, *You think that's hard to get your head around? Let me really blow your minds—eunuchs!*

Small wonder he warned the disciples that they might not get it. It was hard to fit all this together. The dissolution of marriage was wrong because it distorted the "one flesh" picture, but "eunuchs," who weren't in that garden frame at all, had a place in the kingdom of heaven. The redemption story, launching itself from the soil of Eden and arcing through history, was creating a new order of human gender and sexual identity and relationship that would ultimately touch down in the New Jerusalem.

17

Like the Angels

JESUS'S TUSSLE WITH THE Pharisees over divorce presented a convicting challenge for me personally, and not a new one. By the time I was sorting through these questions, later in the summer after that verse from Galatians had popped into my mind on the road to Quarr, my first marriage had long since failed and terminated in divorce. I had gotten married again, to Maggie, who had also been through a bad marriage. Despite our delight in each other, both of us are, to this day, convinced that divorce is not what God intends. We know firsthand just how destructive it is, and how deep the wounds go, especially if, as is the case for us, children are involved. The comments Jesus made about marriage and divorce that the Pharisees and his own disciples found so harsh make good sense to us. We rejoice now in our relationship not because we are able to justify our actions, but because we rest in God's mercy and grace.

If, despite my sinful choices and mistakes, I could believe myself to be accepted and beloved by God, how could I consider people whose fundamental identity gave them no choice but to be rejected by him? It would be narcissistic and hypocritical to think that "there is now no condemnation for those who are in Christ Jesus" (Rom 8:1) applied to me and Maggie, but not to them—wouldn't it?

Thinking about Jesus's comments about marriage in Matthew's gospel reminded me that he had answered another trick question about marriage, posed this time by Sadducees. Roughly speaking, if Pharisees were the religious conservatives of their time, the Sadducees were the liberals. They didn't believe in the resurrection, and in an effort to prove their point, they proposed an absurd situation:

> "Teacher," they said, "Moses wrote for us that if a man's brother dies and leaves a wife but no children, the man must marry the widow and raise up offspring for his brother. Now there were seven brothers. The first one married and died without leaving any children. The second one married the widow, but he also died, leaving no child. It was the same with the third. In fact, none of the seven left any children. Last of all, the woman died too. At the resurrection whose wife will she be, since the seven were married to her?"
>
> Jesus replied, "Are you not in error because you do not know the Scriptures or the power of God? When the dead rise, they will neither marry nor be given in marriage; they will be like the angels in heaven." (Mark 12:18–25)

My first thought, as always when reading this passage, was "That poor woman!" But then I noticed something I had never given much thought to before: when resurrection comes, we won't be married, but "will be like angels." Being like angels could imply a lot of different things, but in the context of this discussion about marriage, it seemed clear to me that Jesus was referencing the idea that they are not gendered as human beings are. Gabriel and Michael are the only two angels named in the Bible; whenever angels show up in the biblical narrative in human form they do so as men—never as women or chubby little boys, despite being commonly depicted that way since the glory days of Renaissance art. The point is not that angels are adult males, but that they are either one gender (which doesn't really make sense: the very point of gender is that it distinguishes one from the other) or without gender at all.

For the first time it occurred to me that Jesus had clearly taught that, when all things were reconciled to God at the end of time, gender would be irrelevant. The complementary joining of male and female as an expression of the nature of God, instituted in the Garden, would be fulfilled by the eradication of the difference—and all the subsequent destructive divisions following the fall—and the joining of one bride to her husband when we arrive in the City.

Jesus would later pray, with the complete understanding of God's character and plan that we lack, "I have given them the glory that you gave me, that they may be one as we are one—I in them and you in me—so that they may be brought to complete unity" (John 17:22, 23a). I had previously thought of this only as a description of a perfect harmony of our mental, emotional and spiritual beings. Probably I've often thought of it as mostly about doctrinal agreement, which—I know!—is ridiculously simplistic. Now it made sense that this "complete unity" would include our physical beings—our gender and sexual identities—as well. In fact, it would include everything. (If anybody could figure out a way for us to be individually distinct and still in "complete unity" it would be the Trinity, wouldn't it?)

I wondered if contemplating these teachings of his Master was what had granted Paul the boldness to write, in a world where wives were chattel to be owned and disposed of, and young boys might be dominated in sexual slavery, that "there is neither . . . male nor female, for you are all one in Christ Jesus." All the differences and divisions that are inherent in or are created by our ethnic, cultural, social and economic identities will also be rendered into one new unity in Jesus—no more Jew or Gentile, slave or free person.

I thought too of how Paul had taught, "Now you are the body of Christ, and each of you is a member of it" (1 Cor 12:27). He taught the same thing to the Romans, Ephesians, and Colossians, as well. Women and men both, members of the *male* body of Christ. His primary point, pretty clearly, was that diversity is a healthy characteristic of, not a barrier to unity—"a body, though one, has many parts, but all its many parts form one body, so it is with Christ" (12:12). A hand, an eye, an ear, a foot—they have distinct functions, but still exist in a fundamental unity. It's a curious image to choose, and amazingly egalitarian when considered in the social context that Paul lived in. There was certainly no ambiguity about the relative identity, roles, or value of men and women in Jerusalem or Rome in his day. Why then, I wondered, would the Spirit prompt him to choose an image in which gender is essentially set aside?

Furthermore, women and men both, according to Paul, are in Christ *sons* of God (Rom 8:14ff.; Gal 3:26)—a position which to be sure emphasizes that every believer is an heir of God, as only males in his time and culture could inherit; but perhaps it was also a way of expressing the irrelevance of gender difference in the kingdom.

If "the body of Christ" was one of the dominant descriptors of the followers of Jesus in Paul's thinking, surely the other was "the bride of Christ"—a rubric also employed by John in the Revelation, culminating in that great vision of the city/bride coming down out of heaven that had got me thinking so differently on the road to Quarr.

"I promised you to one husband, to Christ, so that I might present you as a pure virgin to him," Paul had written to those same Corinthian believers. (I can almost see those Corinthian men squinting, mouths open in embarrassed puzzlement the first time they heard that part of the letter publicly read; 2 Cor 11:2.) In fact, in one astonishing passage, written to the Ephesian church about relationships between husbands and wives, he points out both that "Christ is the head of the church, *his body*," male (5:23; my italics), and describes the church in terms that clearly identify it as his bride, female:

> Husbands, love your wives, just as Christ also loved the church and gave Himself up for her, so that He might sanctify her, having cleansed her by the washing of water with the word, that He might present to Himself the church in all her glory, having no spot or wrinkle or any such thing; but that she would be holy and blameless. (Eph 5:25–27)

It makes perfect sense, then, that Paul wraps up this passage by saying, "This mystery is profound, and I am saying that it refers to Christ and his church"! (5:32) *There's something deep here*, he's saying; *something that, so far, we only understand a little bit about*. It got me pondering where, among the teachings of Jesus, he would have found support for such a revelation.

There are several parables involving wedding feasts, of course, but the bride really isn't the key figure or even directly in the picture in any of them. It's only when you already know that the church is the bride—and none of Jesus's hearers would have, at the time—that the stories make sense in that way.

But there was another clear teaching from Jesus that Paul must have heard passed along by the disciples who were present, although it would be some years yet before John would record it in his gospel.

Imagine the befuddlement of those disciples when, at the Last Supper, Jesus spoke to them as if they were the woman he was engaged to marry one day! Addressing their fears that he was going to leave them behind, he said:

> Do not let your hearts be troubled. You believe in God;
> believe in Me as well. In My Father's house are many
> rooms. If it were not so, would I have told you that I am
> going there to prepare a place for you? And if I go and
> prepare a place for you, I will come back and welcome
> you into My presence, so that you also may be where I
> am. (John 14:1–3)

While it's obscure to many of us today, it would have been crystal clear to the disciples that Jesus was describing his coming actions as those of a bridegroom preparing for marriage. This is hardly new; scholars have long understood the analogy. In those days, once a young man had secured permission to marry the woman of his (or his family's) choice, he announced to his bride-to-be, "I am going to prepare a place for you. I will return when it is ready." Then he'd depart and get to work. "Preparing a place" for his bride meant either renovating and decorating a chamber in dad's house, if it was big enough, or more usually, adding a separate room onto the family domicile. It was the first-century version of newlyweds moving into the basement apartment, except buddy had to frame, insulate, drywall, paint, and broadloom the basement himself for his gal—and it was far more common in Jesus's day than it is now. It was usual for intergenerational families to continue living in the same house indefinitely, and maybe for life.

The bridal chamber, which would become home to the new couple, was called a *chuppah*, and is symbolized to this day at Jewish weddings by a canopy over the bride and groom throughout the wedding ceremony. A wedding wasn't a fifteen-minute ceremony, dinner, and a dance then, either. Bride and groom spent seven days, um, lolling about in that *chuppah*, while the groom's pals made sure they had food, wine, and whatever else they needed. Meanwhile, family and friends cheered them on and partied outside.

I had known all this for years, but with a clearer understanding of the end of the story I thought I now better understood some of the implications of the clues along the way. Here, again, Jesus was offering an unambiguous snapshot of how his beloved followers would have their being once human history had reached its consummation. All of us, including me, an aging straight guy, father of four kids, would be subsumed in the singular and single-gendered bride. We would not "marry or be given in marriage" to each other but be joined to Christ.

Curious, isn't it, that most Christians know that the church is the bride of Christ, but we never consider the gender implications?

I had proposed to myself, when I began to go back through Scripture to see if there was support for the idea that gender would become irrelevant when all was finally redeemed, that as the narrative arc of the great biblical story progressed, I would find clues throughout—and that the clues would become clearer and more numerous the closer it got to the "end." I was also sure that, if the thoughts that popped into my mind on the road to Quarr had any validity, I'd find not only confirmation but some kind of grounding principle or expression in the teaching of Jesus himself. He, after all, is the Word, the supreme articulation of God himself.

I was finding exactly that.

Jesus's teaching about his bride, eunuchs, and us becoming "as the angels" after the resurrection offered a diverse imagery that all expressed the same core concept of the irrelevance of gender in the coming kingdom. And never once, in all his teaching, had he a negative word to say about queer folk. The teaching of Paul and the visions of John picked up, affirmed, and expanded on the teaching of their master. I was becoming more and more convinced that one aspect of the great unity for which Jesus had prayed, the great and ultimate reconciliation of all things to and within their Creator and Redeemer, was the "reconciling" of created gender and sexual difference and sin-induced division into one united mode of being in relationship with the One who loves us and is preparing a place for us.

18

A Kind of Living Prophetic Utterance

THERE ARE THREE GREAT stories of the conversions of individuals in the first part of the Acts. (There's the strange tale of Simon the Sorcerer, too, but we'll set that one aside.) One, of course, is the story of Saul-who-became-Paul, the fire-breathing, hard-line Pharisee who hunted down Christians and arranged for their judicial murder. It's obvious why that story is told: by the time Luke wrote his account, just about everybody in the church across the Roman world knew who Paul was. His conversion was extraordinary—a revelation of and from Christ himself, and evidence that there was nobody Jesus couldn't reach. In a strange way, his background as a Hebrew fundamentalist increased his apostolic cred as the one who would become the evangelist to and theological defender of Gentile Christians. He was such a fascinating character and was having such a profound effect on the growth and trajectory of the church that Luke devoted the last half of his "Acts of the Holy Spirit" to Paul's travels and trials, traveling with him much of the time.

The two other stories bookend the account of Paul's encounter on the Damascus road. There can be little doubt that, from among the thousands of conversion stories available to him, Luke chose these ones because they said something particular about the character of both the gospel and the church.

The conversion of Cornelius, the Roman centurion to whom the Holy Spirit directed Peter (chapter 10, immediately following the account of Saul/Paul's conversion) was such a seismic event that news of it traveled throughout Judea and precipitated a conference of the church in Jerusalem. The idea that a Gentile could "receive the word of God" (11:1) was preposterous and deeply offensive to some. Peter himself admitted that the Holy Spirit had to speak to him in a vision three times before he could be persuaded to go visit this man—not just a Gentile, but a Roman soldier and so the very figure of the pagan regime that oppressed the Jewish people. The message was clear: not only were Gentiles included in the reach of the good news of the kingdom of God, but so were oppressors. Peter and the others can be forgiven for being surprised at this, as Jesus had so clearly focused his words and attention primarily on people who were poor, infirm or oppressed. He had, of course, detoured through the Gentile Decapolis, healing and preaching as he went; he'd drunk the Samaritan woman's water and liberated the demon-possessed man in Gadara, which was also in a Gentile region. Perhaps they remembered him saying to the Syrophoeni-cian woman who begged him to cast a demon out of her daughter, "It is not right to take the children's bread and throw it to the dogs" and forgot that, in the end, he healed the child (Matt 15:26). And there was that Roman centurion and his boy slave.

Later, when Paul and Barnabas got in trouble for making disciples of the Gentiles in Antioch and other Greek cities, Peter humbly defended them, reminding those chapter-and-verse Jewish Christians that he himself had been the first to announce the good news to the Gentiles. Mindful, no doubt, of how hard the Spirit had had to work to convince him at the time, Peter pointed out that "God, who knows the heart, bore witness to them, by giving them the Holy Spirit just as he did to us, and he made no distinction between us and them, having cleansed their hearts by faith" (Acts 15:8, 9). Pretty definitive. "No distinction."

I wonder if Paul remembered those words when he later wrote concerning "the mystery of Christ" to the Ephesians, "This mystery is that the Gentiles are fellow heirs, members of the same body, and partakers of the promise in Jesus Christ through the Gospel" (3:6). There's that mystery again—one body, and the promise of our ultimate union with Christ.

But this is all about Jews and Gentiles. Nobody these days has any trouble imagining us together in the kingdom of God. What does it have to do with queer people? You'll have to follow me a while on this.

Cornelius's personal conversion was also a prophetic event. As a Gentile and a member of the oppressive occupying Roman army, Cornelius himself—his mere presence and being within the community of believers as one of them—was a kind of living prophetic utterance. He made sense of some of the teaching and actions of Jesus, ones that his disciples clearly hadn't given much thought to before. He recalled Jesus's gracious treatment of another Roman centurion, and his affirmation of the man's faith. He fulfilled the words of the Old Testament prophets such as, for instance, Zechariah:

> Sing and rejoice, O daughter of Zion [Jerusalem], for behold, I come and I will dwell in your midst, declares the Lord. And many nations shall join themselves to the Lord in that day, and shall be my people. And I will dwell in your midst. (2:10, 11)

And beyond all that, the presence of Cornelius pointed the way forward. A new reality was emerging, one in which God's "purpose was to create in himself one new humanity out of the two [Jew and Gentile], thus making peace, and in one body to reconcile both of them to God through the cross." By the death of Jesus, God had "destroyed the barrier, the dividing wall of hostility" which kept Jew and Gentile apart (Eph 2:15b, 16; 14b). The old cultural, ethnic, socioeconomic, and religious divisions were being eradicated; Cornelius was living, prophetic testament to the new order God was creating.

The other great conversion story, coming just before Saul's in Luke's telling of it, belongs to the Ethiopian eunuch. Yes, eunuchs again.

The account makes it clear immediately that something special was going on. The Holy Spirit mounted a special mission to save this one man, removing Philip from a busy and very effective evangelistic ministry and sending an angel to cryptically instruct him to "go south to the road—the desert road—that goes down from Jerusalem to Gaza" (Acts 8:26). On his way, Philip met the CFO of the Queen of Ethiopia. He'd pulled his chariot off to the side of the road and was sitting there reading the prophet Isaiah . . .

You know what happened. To cut to the chase, the eunuch believed in Jesus and Philip baptized him in "some water" by the side of the road. Then "the Spirit of the Lord suddenly took Philip away" and he preached his way through all the towns from Azotus to Caesarea. (See Acts 2:26–40 for the entire story.)

From start to finish, the story is at least as extraordinary as the account of the conversion of Cornelius—although Philip, to his credit, didn't argue with the angel or the Spirit as Peter did, and the church didn't have a big row about it afterwards. Presumably because the eunuch went back to Ethiopia. Out of sight, out of mind.

Luke gave the story prime space and treatment though; and reading once again a story I'd heard umpteen times from my childhood on, it seemed clear to me that he did so because this too was a prophetic event, and the eunuch a prophetic figure. Although Luke's gospel doesn't recount Jesus's dissertation on eunuchs and the kingdom of God, his recording of the eunuch's conversion certainly recalls it. Here was proof, in an encounter directly engineered by the Holy Spirit, that Jesus meant what he had said. The kingdom of God *would* be more inclusive than the covenant nation of Israel. The gospel articulated a great leap forward on the narrative arc of God's history of humanity.

If the conversion of Cornelius was a prophetic proclamation that Gentiles and oppressors could also be redeemed and granted citizenship in God's kingdom, the roadside conversion of the Ethiopian eunuch declared a similarly revolutionary message. No one would be barred from that good kingdom because of their gender or sexual identity. Jesus had taught it; the Spirit accomplished it; and now the church—the body of Christ, his bride—witnessed it.

Why did Jesus and the Holy Spirit single out eunuchs to make this point rather than people who were gay or lesbian? I thought it must be because "eunuch" was unquestionably an identity, and one that usually couldn't be altered. (Jesus did describe people who, for the sake of the kingdom, choose a eunuch-like state, presumably one of celibacy and/or childlessness.) "Homosexuality," remember, is a term and concept which only began to have currency in the nineteenth century. Until then, and certainly in the Greco-Roman world, it was thought of as a behavior rather than as an identity. Lifelong, faithful relationships between equals of the same gender were unknown. There was, and still is, lots to disapprove of in the way same-gender sexuality showed up: various forms of domination and manipulation, infidelity, sex as adventurism rather than relationship, and more. Of course, all those things show up in opposite-gender sexuality, too, and are just as wrong when they do.

But all this was just bad behavior; being a eunuch was who you were.

If Cornelius and the eunuch were prophets, in the sense that their extraordinary, Holy Spirit-sanctioned entrances into the kingdom of God fulfilled what the Old Testament prophets had hinted at and Jesus had explicitly taught, and their very beings pointed forward to the nature of the Great Consummation articulated by Paul and envisioned by John—if they were prophets, I realized, so too were people like John, Roxanne, Cassandra, Janice, and dozens of others I've known.

Their presence in my life caused me to question what I thought I knew about God and his kingdom. They pushed me back into the Bible, and shifted my vantage point enough that I began to see familiar passages with fresh eyes and hear the Spirit's voice with newly open ears. Their love for me, and mine for them, softened me up, allowing the Holy Spirit to finally penetrate what had become a hardened crust on the surface of my thinking or perhaps my spirit. Prophets call us to account; they had certainly done that, but prophets also point the way forward, and they did that, too. Because of them, God was able to open my eyes a little so that I could see a bit more clearly what his kingdom will look like. Knowing your destination is crucial to helping you figure out how to get there.

Prophecy, whether it is uttered or embodied, is rarely unambiguous and straightforward. No doubt there are glitches and anomalies in the idea, but perhaps all queer folk are present among us in order to point us to—*to prophetically announce*—the greater reality of the kingdom to come. Among them, the physical constraints of gender identity are broken; a unity of gender in the context of sexual love is portrayed. Most of all, the barriers that separate male from female are breached and shown to be irrelevant. It's far from perfect in our present reality, as are the gospel-proclaimed equalities of ethnic and social condition, but it's there in seed form.

And that greater reality is what we must live toward.

I want to be sure we're clear about this, you and me. As I've noted, the church is predominantly analogized in the New Testament as body and bride. "Body" is about our relationship to each other and the world around us here and now, and is metaphorically male, since it's the body of Christ. The rubric of the body emphasizes diversity in unity. It makes radically clear that females are regarded as having the same value and status as males; different functions in this analogy (a hand, an eye, etc.) are not defined by the actual gender of body members. And every member, regardless of gender or function within the body, is to be honored because "God has composed the body" (1 Cor 12:24).

The metaphor of the bride is about eternal relationship to Jesus, God, and the Spirit, and is metaphorically female in character although both actual genders are included. The bride rubric emphasizes our sameness in belovedness. It's the ultimate fulfillment of Paul's great summation of the redemptive agenda: "There is neither Jew nor Greek, there is neither slave nor free, there is no male and female, for you are all one in Christ Jesus" (Gal 3:28). This is the landing place of the redemptive arc according to the vision John recorded in Revelation 21, where differing restrictive functions and identity markers from "time," including gender, are wiped away along with the tears they have so often prompted.

We are both body and a betrothed bride now, but at the Consummation the long engagement will have run its course and we will become simply his bride, as Jesus, the actual "body," will be present. We, together as one, will be joined to him in an intimacy and unity that will fulfill every longing we've ever known. At last.

If becoming the bride is the goal, then here in the body we should be living toward that now, not trying to return to the Garden. To be clear, we should be living in a way that discards the usual boundaries of gender and sexual identity, just as we should with the usual boundaries of culture, race, power, and privilege. If gender will be irrelevant in determining who will "marry" Jesus someday, should it be relevant now? Is not our transformation, both individually and communally as the people of God, not progressive—grace upon grace? And why should we be surprised if, as human history comes closer and closer to its consummation, male bodies sometimes contain female souls, or vice versa? They may well be pointing the way forward and hinting at that ultimate goal.

Queer folk may still be anomalous in our present world, but prophets have always been anomalies. They wouldn't be prophets otherwise.

Final Words

The Story Isn't Finished Yet

EARLY IN 2017, NOT long after I'd begun writing this book, I hit an emotional wall. It was a slow-motion crash, like those automotive safety clips where you see a close-up of the test dummies as the car rams into the barricade. In fact, when I looked back on it later, I realized it had been coming for years.

It got worse as summer approached and, along with it, a big celebration of Sanctuary's twenty-fifth anniversary we had been planning. I had been there at the beginning, the first full-time worker, and I had been active in one form or another of street-level outreach in Toronto's downtown core for a good fifteen years before that. Throughout Sanctuary's history, I had been the primary pastoral figure, which among other things meant that, almost invariably, I was the one who facilitated the funerals and memorials.

Our community is made up mostly of people who are poor and street-involved. Many are homeless, lots are addicted and/or struggling with mental illness. I would guess that most, to a greater or lesser degree, are afflicted with post-trauma issues. These people were not and are not clients—that's almost a dirty word in our context; they are community members, friends, and even "family" members. One indigenous man calls me "uncle," a term of respect and affection I greatly prize; some others call me "brother" and a few even refer to me as "Dad." Which can be a little strange when coming from someone only a few years younger than oneself, but it's still very sweet.

Because of the poverty and affliction my people experience, the rate of death is absurdly and tragically high. Because of the closeness of relationship, because of the preciousness of these brothers and sisters and the routinely horrid, often violent circumstances in which they pass, their deaths are more than usually traumatic to the community and to me personally. Having had to hold it together so I could properly facilitate the grieving of others, and having had to do that month after month, year after year for a quarter of a century while awash in sorrow myself had, it became clear, done some damage.

I'd wake up in the night assaulted by lurid images of the deaths I'd either witnessed personally or imagined from what I knew about the circumstances of my friends' passing. Lying in my bed in the darkness, they would clip through my mind one after the other like a macabre highlight reel I couldn't shut off. This had happened now and then through the years, but as the anniversary approached, it became a nightly occurrence. I'd come to in the morning exhausted and stunned, feeling as if I had been emotionally pummeled.

At the anniversary celebration itself, I experienced what I would later recognize as my first truly waking dissociative episode. It was triggered by standing with my step-daughter Gillian before the event got underway, watching a montage of photos of members of our community scroll through on a video monitor. I kept saying to her, "He's gone . . . she's dead . . . those two on the left are gone . . ." I had to turn away. I managed to fulfill all my necessary functions that night but felt as though I was watching myself from somewhere up in the rafters, metaphysically and emotionally disengaged. To this day, I can't really remember what happened throughout the rest of that evening.

After a couple of more funerals, and more dissociative episodes that were worse than the first, I knew I needed some help. My wife, Maggie, and my dear friend Alan, Sanctuary's executive director, gave me some good advice about some things I needed to do myself—things I had long been afraid to face—and with their support, I began. But I also thought I needed some good counsel or therapy.

But where to find it? Grief counsellors, I suspected, would be familiar with the struggles of people who had lost a loved one, or maybe even two or three over a short period of time. Trauma therapists generally focused on people who had experienced cataclysmic events in their own lives. What I was experiencing was by no means worse—my dissociative episodes were mild compared to those of some of my friends—but it seemed different: the regular deaths of people I loved, sometimes a few in the course of a single week, dozens upon dozens of them by overdose, suicide, insane accidents, murder; often dying alone in dismal squalid rooms or alleys or parking garage stairwells or cardboard and plastic squats. I didn't know anyone who had been as close to these particular "front lines" for as long as me.

In time I realized that my answer was to be found in the opening chapters of this book: John. John could help me. He had embalmed and buried more than a hundred friends in a short few years at the height of the AIDS crisis, frequently officiating at their funerals. He knew what it was to lose and lose and lose, and in the middle of the loss and the grieving to shepherd others through their own sorrow. I knew he and his husband, Paul, had moved out of the city long since for this very reason—all their friends had died.

Just a few months earlier, I had once again met him over lunch after years of not seeing or communicating with him. John's hair was whiter and he wore a few more lines on his face, but he seemed otherwise little changed. His eyes sparkled with the same good humor. He was generous and gentle and tender without being the least bit maudlin. I'd sent him the chapter that relates some of his story and the effect he had on my own journey, asking for permission to use it in this book and for any editorial comment he might care to offer. That lunch was much like the one we'd shared so long ago: the veil of years and divergent experience dropped away, and it felt like two hearts communed with hardly a filter between.

I called him, told him what was going on, and he answered my request with an enthusiastic, "Of course!" So I began to meet with him regularly, going for a while to their farm for the day, before he and Paul moved to Nova Scotia. Now we see each other through the magic of the internet, although they have a standing invitation from Maggie and me to stay at our place in Toronto whenever they're in town.

It feels, in some ways, as if this quest has come full circle— although not back to the beginning, if that makes any sense. Too far along the story's arc for that now. We're not going back to the Garden. John was a prophet to me, but now he's a pastor, as well. Whatever else that unusual transparency that I experience with him is, I suspect it's also an echo of the unity that will subsume and fulfill us all when we arrive in the City.

May I say a final word to you? If, as a person who seeks better answers, this book hasn't given you a satisfying place to land regarding the place of queer folk in the kingdom of God, I congratulate you on sticking with it all the way through and apologize for not having anything more convincing to offer. I suspect you've hung in there because you really care, and really want better answers than you have yet encountered. May I then encourage you to keep on seeking, asking questions? Remember that the sum total of human understanding is as miniscule within the greater knowledge—and wisdom, grace, mercy, and love—of God as is our own earth within the universe. He is the Great Mystery—and a mystery does not forbid knowledge, but invites us to explore, to venture deep into new territory. Hold what you think you know lightly, knowing that some of it at least will change in time. By all means live according to such knowledge as you believe you have in the moment, as far as you can do so submitting it to the rule of love. For the great, overarching law of the God who is love is that we must love.

If, on the other hand, this book has been helpful to you—well, hurray. I'm glad. Get out there and live, speak, love. Do remember that there are others who want to love as God does, and want to be faithful to him, yet may be stuck as we all are to some degree within the limits of their understanding. Be gracious to them, as you need grace yourself.

If you're queer, I hope this will help increase your confidence in who you are and who your God is and encourage you to live faithfully and joyfully the gospel that proclaims that we are all one in Christ. If you're straight, I guess, really, I hope it does the same for you.

Whoever you are, and whatever your opinion of this book, just remember: the story isn't finished yet.

Acknowledgments

THIS WHOLE BOOK IS, among other things, an acknowledgment of and expression of gratitude toward the lesbian, gay, bisexual, transgender, queer, two-spirited, nonbinary, asexual, and intersex people who have had such a prophetic role in my own life. I'm beyond thankful especially to those who have allowed, with such courage and grace, some small part of their stories to be related herein. There are others, just as courageous and graceful, whose lives have also impacted my own journey in deep ways and for good reasons of their own did not want to see aspects of their lives in print. There must be literally hundreds of individuals whose influence, one way or another, has nudged me gently a little farther along the path that leads homeward, and I'm grateful for each one.

As always, the Sanctuary community in Toronto has been both the place where my deepest lessons have been learned, and where I've been held in the midst of the challenges those lessons have presented. I'm grateful to those street-involved prophets and pastors, to those who anchor the community with their more stable lives, and to those who serve it as staff and board members.

Terri and Miller Alloway have been patrons and encouragers these past fourteen years, as I write this. It's likely that neither this book nor most of the others I've published would have come into being without their generosity. It's worth mentioning that they supported the writing of this book despite being uncomfortable with the subject matter and probably very uncertain about my conclusions; in doing so they have exemplified grace and a deep faith that God knows what s/he is doing. They've also supported my writing buddy, Tim Huff, for whose companionship and encouragement I'm also thankful.

I'm grateful for Michael Clarke, and the formative discussions we've had about these and many other matters over the past thirty years.

My thanks, too, to Rodney, Jim, and the rest of the staff at Wipf and Stock, who gave this book a home (and put the manuscript through its paces) when other publishers wouldn't.

Apart from the Father, Son, and Holy Spirit—to whom be the glory!—there's no one I'm more grateful to and for than my wife, Maggie: challenger, anchor, sounding board, friend, and lover.

Made in the USA
Monee, IL
17 January 2022

89173815R00079